THE CURSE OF THE MASKING-TAPE MUM

$#@%.

A collection of
BASIC INSTRUCTIONS
by Scott Meyer

basicinstructions.net

All Basic Instructions characters
© 2011 Scott Meyer. All Rights Reserved.
What The Duck © Aaron Johnson, used
with permission.

Neither this book nor any portion of it
may be reproduced other than for review
without express written permission of
Scott Meyer, and Don't Eat Any Bugs
Productions. Names, characters, places,
and incidents featured in this publication
either are the product of the author's
imagination or are used fictitiously. Any
resemblance to actual persons (living or
dead), events, institutions, or locales,
without satiric intent, is coincidental.

ISBN 978-098023149-6

From the desk of
Scott Meyer

Two things:

1. This is my third book. I asked Ric to write the foreword to my first book, thinking it would give him a chance at the revenge to which he is so clearly entitled. Instead, he praised me, which I believe proves that he's suffering from Stockholm Syndrome.

I asked my wife Missy to write the foreword to the second book, thinking that if anyone could be counted on to give me the thrashing I deserve, it was her. She was even more complimentary. Clearly, if I'm to ever be brought to justice, I'm going to have to do it myself.

Here are three humiliating facts about me. I once managed to spill an entire Super-Big-Gulp down my own back. In elementary school, I was placed in a class called "Remedial P.E." Back when I was a stand-up comic, on two separate occasions I received "the hook."

Justice is served.

2. While designing the cover for this book I put out a request to several people I respect for quotes, thinking I would put them on the back cover. One of the people I asked, Aaron Johnson, creator of 'What the Duck', wrote "Scott Meyer is an uncontaminated genius who also masquerades as a nice guy. Some may argue that his comic is smart, witty and astute - but 'Basic Instructions' is an undisputed balls-to-the-wall laugh riot. The internet alone can not contain the brilliance of this comic and thanks to the foresight of Johannes Gensfleisch zur Laden zum Gutenberg, we can now enjoy this third treasure-trove of hilarity in book form."

It was very nice of him, but the quote was too large for the back cover. I was about to ask him to make it "less wordy", then I realized that for me to ask anyone to do that would be the very definition of hypocrisy.

He also sent me a great drawing of his duck character dressed as Rocket Hat.

Thanks for buying my book. I hope you enjoy it.

-END TRANSMISSION-

Hostility begets hostility, so a logical first step in making a friend out of an enemy is to treat them like a friend.

Spend time with them. What you think is an antagonistic attitude might be simple discomfort, which may go away in time.

Try to answer any questions, no matter how strange or rude, openly and without getting defensive.

Even if after all your efforts they remain hostile, at least you'll know you tried, which can be rewarding on its own.

This comic came from the observation "There are few gentlemen in a gentlemen's club, there's no glory in a glory hole." I chose not to explore that second part.

2

Never discuss your beliefs at work. Be aware that even light conversation can give clues to your co-workers' beliefs.

I'm really enjoying the "Left Behind" series.

Cool! Are there boobs?

Um, "Left Behind" is a series of books.

So? Some of my favorite books are about boobs.

I don't doubt it.

If someone else does accidentally bring up their deeply held beliefs, do not ever comment on it. Just let the subject die.

They take place after the rapture, when all of the righteous have ascended to heaven and the Earth is populated entirely by sinners.

And then the boobs come out.

Presumably, but I really don't think it's in the book.

Never, ever, under any circumstances make any kind of joke about any of your coworkers' deeply held beliefs.

Oh, I get it. They're hard-core Christian books.

What's that supposed to mean?!

Don't be offended.

"Hard core" is a technical term.

It's used to refer to Christian material where they actually show the Holy Spirit penetrating the soul.

These rules are restrictive, and a little un-American, but if you stray from them you will eventually pay the price.

Congratulations! You managed to offend a Christian and a porn addict with one joke.

It's like hitting a 7-10 split. I should get a trophy or something.

If you like, you could frame your written reprimand.

Wow! We're only two comics and one commentary in, and I gotta say, so far this book is pure filth!

We geeks seem to love asking and answering hypothetical questions, and one of the most often asked ones is:

As this is an exercise in fantasy, you'll be tempted to go big, but choosing a power that's too overwhelming ruins the fun.

The more detailed and specific your choice is, the more fun the ensuing conversation is likely to be.

Choosing a power is only the beginning. The real fun is in discussing how you would use the power once you have it.

 Another good way to answer this question is to clench your teeth, make a fist and say "the power to enforce my will!"

As amazing as they are, modern mobile phones are still made by people, and as such are prone to failure.

My phone's broken.

That fancy one with the MP3 player, video camera, and web browser?

Yeah, it still does that stuff. It just can't make a call.

You never make voice calls anyway.

It's the principle of the thing.

Start by calling your carrier's customer support number. It's the obvious first step and they may be able to help.

I'm locked into my contract for a year, but my warranty ran out two months ago.

That's what the computer says.

What will a new phone cost?

According to the computer, four hundred dollars.

I'm now going to curse at you.

The computer says to expect that.

If your carrier is unable to help, it will be up to you to replace your broken phone.

You had to dig out your old phone? That sucks.

Well, it's a better phone, it just doesn't play MP3s.

So you had to dig out your old MP3 player.

Which isn't so bad. It has way more memory.

Well, I'm sorry you're having to make do with superior equipment.

Once your old phone has been replaced and recycled, get on with your life. After all, it was just a phone.

Still enjoying your new/old phone?

Heck yeah! And the company that made it has a new model coming out with built in GPS, WiFi and a whole new OS!

Haven't you learned anything?

Yes, I've learned that I'm a weak, weak man.

Many idiots are just smart enough to know they're idiots. They try to keep you from noticing by telling made-up stories.

One time back when I was a hard-boiled detective I was chasing this perp ...

You were a detective?!

Yup.

Specifically, a "hard-boiled detective"?

The hardest ... boiled.

Confronting them is one possible course of action. You can also entertain yourself by pressing them for more bogus details.

What was it like?

Not that glamorous. Mostly just tracking down adulterers and insurance cheats.

Which one was the guy you were chasing?

Both. He claimed he was injured when his mistress fell on him.

By the same token, if they make a factual error you can correct them, or you can allow them to build on it.

I knew where to look for him because I had studied his moo.

"Moo"?

It's detective lingo. Stands for "mode of operation." It means his habits.

Couldn't you abbreviate that as M.O.?

Which you'd pronounce as "moo."

I suppose you would.

It may seem cruel to milk someone for entertainment, but remember, they started by insulting your intelligence.

I woke up in the hospital.

Did he shoot you?

No, he picked up his mistress and threw her at me.

That would fit his moo.

One-sided conversations are never fun. If both parties were interested in the conversation, it wouldn't be one-sided.

The most common method to end a one-sided conversation is to be silent. This works immediately, or until you break.

Another method is to engage in the conversation in an effort to make it more interesting. This never works.

The only way to end it is to make the other person want it to end by steering it to a topic they don't want to discuss.

In this age of digital downloads, it is rare to procure an entire album of music at once. When you do, make the most of it.

If the album came on a CD, take a moment to look at the cover and liner notes. They're part of the experience.

Upon your first listen-through of the album, you will invariably form some superficial first impressions.

Keep listening. Repeated listenings give you more subtle insights, and a greater appreciation of the artist's intent.

 The album cover is actually just a single Photoshop layer from a drawing of Mullet Boss. Also, I'm proud that I had the willpower to avoid a boner pun.

In fan fiction (or "fanfic"), new stories are created using characters from existing works, by fans of the original.

I have this great idea for a story about the A-Team.

Do they help a guy who's mentally stuck in the 80s?

When writing fan fiction, stick to the original work's format. The idea is to honor the original, not mangle it.

Some squatters hire the A-Team because the guy who owns their squat is trying to evict them.

But ... I think the landlord's totally within his rights.

Exactly! It's morally ambiguous.

Yes. If there's one thing the A-Team is remembered for, it is its moral complexity.

That said, feel free to throw in a twist they couldn't or wouldn't have done on the original. You are the writer, after all.

So to fight the A-Team, the landlord hires the Equalizer! Try to tell me you wouldn't want to read that story!

I'd want to read it. I just wouldn't want anyone to see me reading it.

Clive Cussler's entire career is built on that same foundation.

Pander to what fans would want to see, but bear in mind that not everyone wants to see the same things you do.

So'd you read it?

Yeah, and I could have done without the scene where McCall and B.A. ... um ...

Make sweet, sweet love?

I also didn't like you constantly referring to it as "making sweet, sweet love."

I refuse to write a sex scene with no emotional component. Sue me.

I'm pretty sure someone will.

How to Help Someone Improve Their Plan

Other people are always making plans. Sometimes those plans involve you.

> **Did you get my e-mail?**

> **Yeah, but why did you send it to me?**

> **I need you to clean it up and send it on official stationery.**

> **Your suggestion to Mythbusters? You really think that's the best use of a skilled employee's time?**

> **No, that's why I'm having you do it.**

Because you didn't formulate the plan, you may see problems that the planner did not due to their personal biases.

> **Dear Mythbusters. Please test the myth that a dude's voice gets higher after he has been kicked in the junk. Please test it on Jamie.**

> **Wow! There's nothing a guy with a moustache hates more than a guy with a much better moustache.**

If you do see a need to change the plan, do so respectfully, and give the plan's originator the final say. It is their plan.

> **Instead of "dude," I wrote "man."**

> **Fine.**

> **For "junk," I put "groin."**

> **Whatever.**

> **And instead of "cute redhead," I said they should use a robot leg.**

> **Hmmmm. Make it a "sexy-lady robot leg."**

> **If I must.**

Taking the back seat can be frustrating, but when the plan comes to fruition, you will be proud that you had a hand in it.

> **I can't believe they took his suggestion!**

> **I can't believe Grant made such a convincing sexy-lady robot leg!**

> Whoosh

> KLANG

> OOF!!

> **Well, I suspect he had that laying around from an earlier project.**

Got a nice tweet from Mythbuster Grant after this ran. Makes me feel good when someone proves they have a sense of humor, after I imply they build sex-robots.

Running into an old acquaintance often results in an awkward conversation.

Start by talking about old times. Remembering the times when you saw each other often sparks conversation.

Failing that, move on to what you and your acquaintance have been doing in the intervening time.

When the conversation has run its course, give your acquaintance a way to stay in touch with you in the future.

How to Totally Change the Appearance of a Major Character in a Comic Strip

There are many reasons to change a character's appearance. Perhaps you only drew the character in three poses, and it is making writing natural dialog difficult.

And for some reason, it's not possible to draw more poses without substantially changing the look of the character.

If the change is necessary, do it as soon as possible. Put thought into it and do it right so you won't have to do it again.

When the redesign is complete, unveil it to your readers. Pay close attention to any feedback you receive.

So, yeah. I work from photos, and only got three poses from Ric. Then he changed his hair and his clothes. Luckily his defeatist attitude remained.

12

How to Tell If Someone Is Dangerously Crazy

First, let me say that I believe everybody is a little crazy. Seriously. Everybody.

CRAP!

CRAP!

CRAP!

You know, one definition of insanity is to keep doing the same thing while expecting a different result.

How many times have you told me that?

Hundreds.

Has it ever changed my behavior one bit?

CRAP!

But occasionally someone will make you wonder if they are crazy in a way that could lead to personal injury for you.

I've started collecting knives!

I've started concealing my terror behind a forced smile!

As soon as you suspect someone's a danger, take steps to protect yourself.

Why're you standing so far away?

No reason. How long are your arms?

A couple feet.

And how long's the blade of that knife there?

Seven inches. Why do you ask?

I'll tell you after I've backed up another foot.

Once you're safe, investigate as best you can to discover if they are harmless, or if they should be avoided in the future.

Standing that far away'll only save you if your assailant doesn't have a throwing knife.

They make such a thing?

I've got one right here. Wanna see it?

Sure, I'll go get my binoculars.

Oh, and also, Ric started collecting knives! Probably would have changed my portrayal of him if I hadn't already moved to the far side of the continent.

Address your captive. Make sure he knows that he is totally at your mercy.

> Once again, Rocket Hat, you have fallen into the clutches of the Moon Men! This time you'll find escape quite impossible. Rather than simply cut your chin-strap, we have taken the liberty of removing it entirely!

> I could just take his hat.

> That'd be a bit too obvious, don't you think?

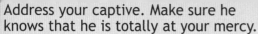

Tell your captive what you plan to do to him. Anticipation of his agonizing demise will be as torturous as the demise itself.

> Now I will have you shot with the Stun Ray. And it will be set on "kill!"

> Why not just shoot him with the Kill Ray?

> You just don't understand subtlety at all, do you?

Once you have had your fill of gloating, leave the actual dirty work to a trusted minion, rather than exert yourself.

> Listen! Subtlety makes us seem unpredictable and intelligent, making us even more terrifying.

> Fine, I'll shoot him with the Kill Ray subtly.

> THERE'S NO SUBTLE WAY TO SHOOT A MAN WITH A &%$@ING KILL RAY!

Now all that's left is to wait for your faithful lackey to report how it went.

> Emperor! Rocket Hat flew away.

> How is that possible with no chin-strap?!

> He held on to the hat by its brim.

> The hat has no brim!

> Yes it does sir, It's very small and subtle.

> SEE!! THAT'S WHAT I'M TALKING ABOUT!!

I think this is the first appearance of the current Moon-Man uniform, which consists of saftey glasses and footy pajamas with the Moon-Man logo.

When planning your retirement, be sure to prepare for the worst case scenario.

I plan to work until I'm retirement age, then die two weeks later, leaving my wife to live off of the insurance policy.

That's pretty grim, isn't it?

Yeah I guess.

The idea of being married to the same woman for that long a time!

Uh, that's the least grim part of the plan.

But don't assume that the worst will happen. Indeed, your retirement years could be among the best of your life.

I'm gonna buy me a camper and a dog, and I'll just drive around the country camping. I've always loved nature.

What better way to show it than to spend your golden years aimlessly burning fossil fuels?

Plan thoroughly. You'll never think of everything, but feeling prepared is the next best thing to being prepared.

I'd also need to get a shotgun. In case anyone gives me any trouble.

Define "trouble."

Oh, you know. Robbing me. Hassling me. Looking at me cockeyed.

I see your plan. Prison as a nursing home! Very clever!

Now that you have a solid plan, you can look forward to your retirement with a greater sense of confidence.

So that's our future. A deceased benefactor and a lone vigilante.

I won't necessarily be alone. Your wife will be available.

She hates camping ... and you.

Oh.

She might watch your dog for you while you're in the joint.

Well, that's something.

One of these two plans is, in fact, the actual retirement plan of a friend of mine. I'd ask you to guess which, but either way's kind of a bummer.

How to Beat the Heat

Hot weather is uncomfortable, and can be dangerous, but you can't let heat keep you from doing things you enjoy.

Come on. We're going to the outlet mall.

Nah, it's an open air mall, and it's way too hot today.

If you let warm weather stop you, it'll be months before we go to the outlet mall.

Heartbreaking.

Wear clothing that will minimize your discomfort and help keep you cool.

This hat will keep the sun out of my eyes, and the sweat from rolling down my face.

And this shirt's bright color and loose weave will reflect heat, and allow for the flow of air and odors.

Odors?

YES! Especially if I stand like this.

Which I will.

It is extremely important that you stay hydrated. Drink plenty of water.

Are you gonna drink that whole thing at the mall?

I'm gonna drink it in the car. I'll need to refill it at the mall.

You'll be peeing constantly.

If staying hydrated means spending more time in the air-conditioned bathroom, then that's the price I'll have to pay.

There's no one way to defeat the negative effects of hot weather, but doing lots of little things can add up.

I'm sorry Scott, but I just don't want to be seen in public with you looking like that.

So, you're saying I have to stay home?

Yes.

Heartbreaking.

How to Prevail in a Battle of Wills

Few people seek conflict, but from time to time even the most docile of us will become engaged in a battle of wills.

The cat's throwing up. The first of us to get up should clean it.

You basically just challenged me to a "Not getting up off your butt" contest.

gump gump gump

Hmmmm. My victory does seem unlikely.

A battle of wills is, by definition, mental. Intimidate your opponent, and make them fear that victory is impossible.

PFFT! All I've gotta do is sit here doing nothing longer than he does. How hard can that be?

ZZZZZZ

Oh, he's good.

Of course, if they're a worthy opponent, they will still put up resistance.

BDAH! What the hell!

What? I just put on American Idol.

You know I can't sleep with American Idol on. It gives me nightmares.

You've never told me what the nightmares are about.

Me watching American Idol.

Of course, you don't really win a battle with your will alone. You win with your will, your skills and your wits.

If you're that sleepy, you should go to bed.

You're right.

And since you're up, you can clean the cat barf.

HA! It wasn't a "sitting on your butt" contest. It was a "sitting on your butt, thinking" contest.

I never had a chance.

I have never found another use for the drawing of me in the last panel. Please, do not take that as a challenge.

17

To those of us who were cursed with an awkward wave, the development of an alternative gesture is imperative.

Take a good look at how you wave to see if you can easily correct the problem.

If your wave cannot be salvaged, try exploring other gestures that are recognized as a form of greeting.

Don't get fancy. The more interactive and idiosyncratic your greeting is, the more likely it is to be misconstrued.

People need something to strive for. Therefore, it is mentally healthy to set lofty but realistic long-term goals.

Gentlemen, I intend to set a world record.

This should be good.

I plan to construct the world's largest book of world records!

Yup, that should have been good.

Even the loftiest goal is nothing without a solid, realistic plan for achieving it.

I'll just take the largest current book of world records and add one page with one record on it!

That's pretty lazy, isn't it?

I wanna set a record. I don't necessarily want to put a lot of effort into it.

Fair enough.

Analyze your reasons for achieving this goal, and make sure they are righteous.

Why would you do this?

To see their reaction.

That would be pretty sweet.

Hey, you've said two things I've agreed with!

I think that may be a record all its own!

Once your task is complete, you will feel a well-earned sense of satisfaction that will last you the rest of your life.

Six Months Later:

The new book of world records is out.

Did his plan work?

Kinda. They added two new records. "Biggest book of records," which they took themselves. And "laziest attempt at a world record."

YOU DID IT!

Victory never felt more humiliating.

These two guys are the founders of Jet City Improv in Seattle. They are great guys who heard a lot of usless ideas from me over the years.

Collecting things can be a great hobby. It combines the thrill of the hunt, the flush of victory, and the fun of human greed.

... a buck knife, three lock blades and a big bowie knife like Brock Samson's.

Sounds like you're really enjoying your knife collection.

Oh yeah! Do you collect anything?

Knife-resistant garments.

Don't say too much about your collection unless you're sure the person you're talking to shares your enthusiasm.

What do you do with all those knives? Just sit around cutting stuff?

I do a lot more with my knives than just cut!

I brandish. I wield. I secrete them about my person.

Frankly, I was happier thinking you just cut stuff.

You don't have to collect physical objects. Train spotting and bird watching are examples of collecting experiences.

I believe when you eat something you add its strength to your own.

I have the strength of one hundred and thirty eight chickens and four whole cows.

No pigs?

No. I keep kosher.

Others may not understand your choice of items to collect or your enjoyment of your collection. Don't let that stop you.

Hey, guess what!

Please don't tell me you bought another useless garment.

My new chain-mail gloves aren't useless. They're knife-resistant, for one thing!

I own every item in the last panel except for the knife-proof gloves. Just a little window into my life that you did not need.

A good story often finds the protagonist in a situation that is extraordinary, but easily understood by the listener.

Be specific in your descriptions. The details are what make your tale come alive in the mind of the listener.

The protagonist of your story should be sympathetic, but if the story's about you, be careful not to sound self-serving.

Stories should, when possible, include a big finish. If necessary, organize the story so the best part is held for last.

Even if you've known someone for years, you can still learn something that makes you see them in a new light.

Back when I had my pacemaker put in ...

You have a pacemaker?! That's so cool!

What's cool? That I have heart disease, or that there's a treatment?

I think something about you is cool. Why not just leave it at that.

It may take some effort to process the new information and integrate it into your image of the person.

I just didn't know you were a cyborg.

Please don't call me a cyborg.

I could call you a Guyborg.

No.

Mandroid?

No.

Man-chine?

No.

RoBart?

Maybe if my name was Bart, but everyone knows it isn't.

True. Everyone does know that.

In the long run, you'll find that the more information you have about someone, the better you'll understand them.

Lots of things make sense now that I know that you're more machine than man.

Seriously, a pacemaker is a tiny little machine.

Yes, but you're not much of a man.

Though they may seem different, they are the same person they always were. You changed, not them. You've learned.

It's not like having a pacemaker gives me powers.

But does it give you any weaknesses?

Well, I'm told some microwave ovens can interfere with it ... I shouldn't have told you that.

Nonsense!

Say, what are your lunch plans? If you like I could run out and get you a Hot Pocket.

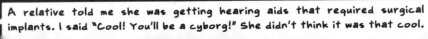

A relative told me she was getting hearing aids that required surgical implants. I said "Cool! You'll be a cyborg!" She didn't think it was that cool.

The Drill Sergeant method of teaching is all about dominance. It is imperative that you shame your pupil immediately.

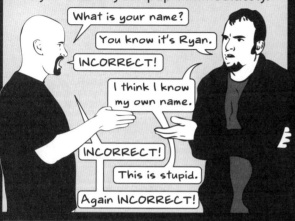

What is your name?

You know it's Ryan.

INCORRECT!

I think I know my own name.

INCORRECT!

This is stupid.

Again INCORRECT!

Keep your pupil off-balance by punishing them for even the slightest infraction. Make up infractions if you must.

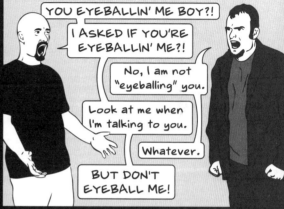

YOU EYEBALLIN' ME BOY?!

I ASKED IF YOU'RE EYEBALLIN' ME?!

No, I am not "eyeballing" you.

Look at me when I'm talking to you.

Whatever.

BUT DON'T EYEBALL ME!

Once your pupil is utterly cowed, show them a more human side. Make it clear that you're doing this for their benefit.

Look, sorry that I come off as gruff and hostile. It's just so important that you remember...

...not to eyeball me.

Once you've broken down their defenses, you can impart your training with total confidence that the lessons will stick.

You're supposed to be training me how to log on to your stupid company's stupid web site, STUPID!

Indeed. Your username is "incorrect." Your password is "eyeball."

So, you were verbally abusing me to make it more memorable.

Yes. It's what educators call a "win-win."

In any ongoing narrative, there will be characters and situations that will lend themselves to becoming a spin-off.

I've been reading the comments on your comic strip. It seems like I have quite a following.

Indeed! Me abusing you makes the readers happy.

Maybe you could do a spin-off for my character. You know, give me the respect I deserve.

The respect you deserve. I can do that.

YAY!

Yay indeed.

The spin-off must be kept separate and distinct from the original in order to have its own identity and style.

Scott Meyer

presents:

Basic Instructions'

"Rick"

by Scott Meyer

Episode I
"Time to Lose"

That said, it should be similar in tone and sensibility to the original narrative.

I am future Rick. I have come to tell you about the future ... Rick.

Yes?

In my time, we've been divorced five times and have one plastic testicle.

Only one? Awesome!

If the spin-off fails, you can reintegrate the spin-off's characters and story line back into the original plot.

Turns out people don't want to hear about your testicle.

Testicles.

Whatever. People don't care about it.

Them!

Dude, drop it.

YOU BROUGHT IT UP!!

Heh, don't you mean I brought them up?

GAHHH!

Rather than create a brand new legend, it's easier to simply modify an existing one people already find believable.

Of course Walt Disney wasn't really frozen. That technology belongs to Col. Sanders.

WHAT?!

They shuttle his frozen corpse from KFC to KFC, keeping him in the walk-in freezer to hide him from his many enemies.

And the health department.

Bolster your urban legend with as many irrelevant coincidences as possible. Refer to these coincidences as "evidence."

That's why they changed the name to KFC.

"Kovertly Frozen Colonel."

Covertly is spelled with a C.

Yes, they've covered their tracks well.

Incorporate existing rumors to make your story jibe with what the general public perceives as reality.

I'd heard they changed their name because they've been using genetically modified birds that the FDA wouldn't let them call chickens.

Nah, it has nothing to do with that.

So, you're not denying the existence of eight-legged chickens?

Of course not! I'm not a nut!

Nothing short-circuits the brain like fear. Make your urban legend so terrifying that they'll be afraid to not believe it.

The Colonel shall rise again, and his obedient army of Octo-Chickens will emerge from their bucket and serve us all some extra crispy righteousness!!

You seem to know an awful lot about this.

INDEED! FOR I HAVE EATEN THE SLAW!!

JOIN US!! IT'S FAMILY STYLE DINING!!!

After I wrote this, I spent about a week loudly declaring that I had "eaten the slaw". My wife is a lucky, lucky woman.

Many classic monsters are exaggerated male archetypes. That's why both women and men can relate their stories.

Ah, she's getting away.

AGH! SHE'S GETTING AWAY!

Frankenstein's monster, for example, was an oaf who inadvertently hurt those around him, often without knowing how.

You pretty.

Thank you.

Almost pretty as your sister.

You $%¢#.

What? Just saying. Want to hump you. Or sister.

You son of a ¢%@#!!

You AND sister?

Dr. Jekyll was a well-mannered, decent, civilized man until a chemical substance brought out all of his worst tendencies.

Dreadfully sorry for my behavior last night. It was just the serum talking, you see?

Perhaps you should stop drinking the serum, then.

Don't try to change me, baby. That's the serum's job.

Zombies want only one thing and will pursue it relentlessly and mindlessly.

Brains.

Brains.

At least you want me for my brains.

By brains I meant boobs. It was a euphemism.

Euphemism.

Euphemism.

In retrospect, Frankenstein's Monster's dialog is a bit awkward. It's hard to do witty repartée while talking like a caveman ... about "humping".

As I stated in part one, many classic monsters are based on male behavior patterns so that they'll be relatable.

How can you possibly identify with the monster? He's a brutish creep who chases innocent women so he can do unspeakable things to them.

You know what? Never mind.

He also has hair on his back.

Vampires remorselessly use their victims to get what they want and discard what remains of them when they are satisfied.

Just so you know, you'll be paying for dinner, And when we go back to your place I won't be spending the night. I sleep alone.

Well let's just skip to the best part of the evening.

Us going back to your place?

You going home.

The Blob was a soft, moist, all-consuming mass that filled all open space, and in the process smothered those in its way.

Today I'm having lunch with a few friends.

Great! I'd love to meet your friends. What're we doing after that?

Getting a pedicure.

That'll be fun! Then what are we doing?

Breaking up.

Can we still be friends?

Sure.

Cool! What're we doing after that?

The Creature from the Black Lagoon was a mouth-breathing loner who stalked prey from afar, then attacked clumsily.

I've been watching you for a long time, and

‑gasp‑smack‑gasp‑

I was wondering if you'd like to

‑pant‑gasp‑

get groped by a mouth-breather.

No thanks?

I get it. You're

‑gasp‑smack‑

stuck up

How to Tell What Kind of Monster You Are Dating: Vol. 3

As I've been pointing out, many famous monsters are simply exaggerations of stereotypical male behavior patterns.

> We appear to be dying from a virus that would give you a mild cold.

cough cough

> Typical.

King Kong was way more interested in his girlfriend than she was in him, which caused him to become possessive.

> I'd like to see other people.

> Fine. I'll hold you up higher so you'll have a better view.

The Fly started out as a gifted scientist and turned into a totally different creature. A filthy, annoying creature.

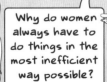

> I don't complain when you talk with your mouth full, and I don't complain when you clip your toenails in the living room, but I really wish you wouldn't do them both at the same time.

> Why do women always have to do things in the most inefficient way possible?

Mad Scientists alienate themselves from humanity by focusing solely on work that only they understand and appreciate.

> You know, Scott, it's been a while since we've gone out to dinner.

> I can't tonight. I'm too busy writing this joke about how guys who criticize their girlfriends' clothing are a lot like Mothra.

When frustrated with your communal workplace, co-workers may discuss their issues with you, thinking you share them.

You know what my biggest mistake was in this job?

Applying for it?

No, after that.

Showing up on the first day?

After that.

Assuming that I care about your problems?

No, before that.

Asking the occasional question will make you appear interested without really getting you involved in their problems.

I let the boss know that I'm smarter than he is. Now he feels threatened and is constantly taking it out on me.

How'd you let him know that you're smarter than him?

I told him.

Yup. That was a mistake.

If you do have some new insight into their dilemma that can alleviate their problems, don't hesitate to offer it.

Maybe it's not that he knows you're smarter and feels threatened. Maybe it's that he knows you think you're smarter and he's offended.

So what you're saying is that he can't handle reality!

Well, that's what you're hearing, at any rate.

Just don't assume that your coworker will understand or follow your advice.

So what should I do? Tell him I've suffered brain damage, and now I'm slightly dumber than he is?

YES! You should tell him exactly that! But wait an hour before you tell him.

To give me time to think of the right wording?

No, to give me time to get my video camera.

A co-worker told me once that the boss feared his superior intelligence. He added that his mom agreed with him. Who was I to call his mom a liar?

29

Few things cause others to have friendly feelings for you quite like sharing heartwarming tales of your childhood.

We didn't have much money, but mom would bring things home from work that she thought would make good toys.

Aw, that's so sweet!

She made false teeth for a living.

I withdraw my previous statement.

Throw in little details about your family members that will make them seem more relatable to your audience.

It was mostly loose teeth and plaster casts of diseased mouths. She had one upper-jaw cast she used as an ashtray.

That's horrifying!

She painted flowers on the jaw to make it look less disturbing.

It didn't work.

Wrap up your story with the valuable life lesson you learned from the situation.

That's the kind of thing that could give you a life-long fear of dentists.

Actually, it gave me a fear of not going to the dentist. No matter what the dentist wants to do, I just picture my mom grinding a cigarette out on my palate and it doesn't seem that bad in comparison.

A good heartwarming tale will entertain your audience at the time, and may stick with them for the rest of their lives.

You should send that story to the American Dental Association's marketing director.

Why? Do you think they'd buy it from me?

Sure! If only to keep you from telling it again.

ALL TRUE! THE PLASTER CASTS, TRUE! THE ASHTRAY, TRUE! She made me a D&D dice that appeared to be made of gums! Wish I still had 'em.

One common method of psyching out an opponent is to brag about yourself, which is pathetic, and easily ignored.

Were you aware that I rock?

Why no, I wasn't.

Strange that I would know you for over a decade without ever finding that out.

Other methods are more brutal, leaving you with no alternative but to retaliate.

I hereby offer unto you THE WHAMMY, which, as you know, is unbeatable.

Indeed, unless I make with the double whammy.

NO! Please don't make with that!

Too late! It's already been made with.

This will lead your foe to retaliate, resulting in a psych-out vicious cycle. A "Vicious Psych-le," if you will.

I'm afraid you leave me no option but the rare and devastatingly effective ... triple whammy.

How is such a thing possible?

You'll see, just as soon as I find a roll of duct tape.

Mind games can suck the fun out of the real game. Often the best plan is not to play with a psych-out artist at all.

Quad-whammies all around. Stalemate! But, how can we play the game without dropping our guard?

I propose that we roll the dice by sucking them into our mouths and spitting them onto the board.

Know what? You win.

I ROCK!

Often we all find ourselves faced with a decision that has no clear resolution.

I can either waste money on expensive refill cartridges for my razor, or I can waste our natural resources by buying cheap disposable razors.

Or you can waste your time standing here obsessing over your shaving equipment.

Look seriously at all of your options, weighing their various pros and cons.

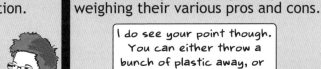

I do see your point though. You can either throw a bunch of plastic away, or throw money away.

I could say "screw it" and grow a big bushy biker beard.

Then you'd be throwing your marriage away.

If you still can't decide, discuss the situation with someone who may see the problem from a different perspective.

You shave?

Are you kidding? I shave the sides and back of my head, my neck and my cheeks every morning.

Wow! That's a lot of trouble to go to just to look like a bald dude with an outdated beard.

Eventually you will have to make a decision. Indecision can be much more damaging than making the wrong choice.

I've decided I'm gonna switch to disposable razors.

So you figure saving money's more important than saving our planet's resources, eh?

No, I just realized that my money is a resource as well.

A relatively scarce resource at that!

Quite.

When you think about the sheer amount of crap people say to you every day, it's no surprise that you mis-hear some of it.

I need you to make an appointment for me.

Sure thing. What for?

Bag wag sing.

I'm sorry, I mis-heard you.

I hope.

Ask them to repeat what they said, exactly as they said it the first time. Changing the wording is not helpful.

I'm sorry, what was that?

My bag.

Wags.

Yes.

Uh, okay.

WAG SING! WAG SING, MY BAG!

I still don't know what you're talking about, but I'm begging you to stop explaining.

If you still don't understand, tell them what you heard. This tells them why you look confused, and will be amusing.

If I hear you right, you want me to schedule you an appointment to go somewhere and sing while you wag ... your, uh ... your bag.

That's insane!

I know, right! You don't make an appointment for that kinda thing!

You just show up and make sure there are no cops around!

Keep trying until you understand. The embarrassment of admitting not hearing them is better than making a mistake.

BACK ... WAXING! I want you to make me an appointment to get my back hair waxed! Do you understand me now?

No, and I never will!

 Every now and then I finish a comic and think to myself "nobody's gonna like this but me." This time I was thinking it before I was half way done.

No civilized person would ever attack someone without warning. Declare your intentions to do your opponent harm.

This is it, Rocket Hat. I shall dispatch you as all civilized tyrants dispatch their foes. By killing you myself!

With my pinkies fully extended.

Anything less would be gauche.

For combat to be civilized, each combatant must have a sporting chance, and that means rules.

We shall do battle in the traditional Moon-Man manner.

Hmm. Man-Manner.

Moon-Man-Ner.

Nah, sounds too much like "Moon-Manure."

Anyhoo, you'll be armed with a battle spatula. Good luck with that.

The rules should be carefully designed so the odds are as balanced as possible.

The spatula is made of pure Moon-Lead, which is vastly superior to Earth-Lead, in that it is heavier and breaks more easily.

The traditional Moon-Man way of fighting is often described as "unfair."

Once the fight has begun, use all of your skill and cunning to prevail. To do less would be dishonorable.

I'm sorry you lost, Sire, but you must admit it was quite impressive how he used the battle spatula to flip you over and then press out your juices.

Indeed. Moon-Intelligence failed to discover that Rocket Hat had worked at McDonald's in high school.

 Any Food Network host will tell you that you shouldn't press the juices out of a hamburger patty. If the Emperor fights Bobby Flay, bet on the Emperor.

No matter how smart the people in your life are, occasionally someone will say something that is just objectively wrong.

> I think Twilight is the best book ever written about vampires.

> I disagree with every part of that sentence.

> Starting with when you said, "I think."

Explain as calmly and rationally as you can why they are wrong.

> Twilight is not about vampires.

> Half of the characters are vampires!

> Can they turn into bats?

> No.

> Does sunlight hurt them?

> No, but they do drink blood!

> That doesn't make them vampires. They are leech-men at best.

Once you've proven they are wrong, explain why it's important to be right. Make them care as much as you do.

> Leeches do glisten a bit in bright sunlight.

> So what if Stephenie Meyer did change all the stupid, made up vampire rules?

> Why do you care?

> Because she's lowering our standards! Every Halloween from now on we'll have people claiming to be dressed as vampires because they sprayed on some body glitter and didn't wash their hair!

Be prepared for the fact that setting someone straight seldom makes them like you more, or want to talk to you.

> And now that she's screwed up vampires, there's no telling what she'll mess with next!

> She could make something crazy, like werewolves that change at will and don't fear the full moon.

> I'm sorry. I am getting outta hand here. I don't think we should discuss Twilight anymore.

> Um, agreed.

  Twilight's got vampires and wolfmen. I'd like to see her take on the Gill-man. He'd be a good looking Olympic swimmer with a slight greenish complexion.

35

Sometimes we all need to take some medication. It's important to be sure that any drug you take is worth the risk.

My doctor put me on anti-depressants!

What took him so long?

First he had me try to avoid the things that depress me.

I haven't noticed you avoiding things, but I haven't seen you much lately.

No. You haven't.

Look objectively at the benefits of taking the drug. Not just the promised benefit, but the benefit you actually receive.

My doctor put me on anti-depressants!

Uh, yeah. How's it going?

I'm happy with the results.

You've been planning that joke for a while.

Yup!

And that doesn't depress you at all?

Nope!

The pills must be working.

No matter how positive the benefits are, you must take an equally serious look at the drug's drawbacks.

My doctor put me on anti-depressants!

Say, is one of your anti-depressant's side effects short term memory loss?

How did you know?!

I know many things. Like that your new anti-depressant can cause memory loss.

WOW! How'd you know?!

Now objectively weigh the drug's benefit against the drawbacks and decide if the medication is worth it to you.

My doctor put me on anti-depressants!

Yeah yeah. Whatever.

You know, if these anti-depressants work by making you forget that you're depressed, that just sorta seems like cheating.

But if I'm happy, does that matter?

That's a good point. What's the name of this drug?

I don't remember.

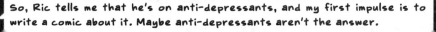

So, Ric tells me that he's on anti-depressants, and my first impulse is to write a comic about it. Maybe anti-depressants aren't the answer.

Men of great prowess are often prone to prideful boasting of said prowess.

I'm taking my girlfriend out to dinner tonight for her birthday.

I hope she has a happy birthday.

I'm gonna make sure she does. Guess how.

I'd rather not.

I'm gonna have sex with her.

Sadly, that is what I'd have guessed.

Vague, empty boasting impresses nobody. Offer quantifiable metrics to describe the magnitude of your prowess.

Seriously. I am a monster in the sack. In fact, no woman I've ever been with has ever come back for seconds.

One time with me is enough.

That certainly is evidence of your ... monstrousness.

Eventually, it'll be time to demonstrate your prowess. If you've refrained from exaggeration, you have nothing to fear.

All right. That's good.

Yeah. It is good.

No, really. Get off.

I am getting off!

GET OFF YOU &%#$!

GET OFF!

I appreciate your encouragement.

Once you've fully demonstrated your prowess, talk of it will no longer be seen as boasting, but discussion of fact.

She kept shrieking "get off, get off." And then I got off. All the way off.

But was she, uh, satisfied?

She seemed happy, but of course all of my lady friends seem happy when I'm done.

I don't doubt it.

This is the most controvercial strip I've ever done. When I wrote the third panel, the female character's voice was laughing in a good-natured, (Cont)

In order to capitalize on an upcoming technology, you must see it coming in the first place. Keep your eyes open.

I read today that scientists at Ohio University found a cheap, plentiful source of hydrogen.

It's something you deal with every day.

Hot air? Boredom? Idiocy?

You're on the right track.

Am I really?

Don't be afraid to share information. Others may have insights you lack, or at the very least offer moral support.

IT'S URINE!

I get it! I was on the right track because it's something you produce lots of.

Yeah, I thought I'd give you that one.

Thank you.

Try to think of possible uses for the new technology. Don't be afraid to think big.

Imagine if every car was powered by urine-derived hydrogen. We wouldn't be dependent on oil, cities would be quieter, the air would be cleaner because the cars' only exhaust would be water so clean you could drink it.

But would you drink it?

Hell no! It used to be pee!

Think of ways that you can get out ahead of the new technology. Be aware that you might experience some resistance.

If someone stockpiled

You're not collecting your urine.

Of course not. One man could never produce

Allow me to rephrase that. You're not collecting OUR urine.

Drat.

(Cont) but irritated way. Several readers didn't see it that way, and expressed disappointment that I'd write a comic condoning rape. (Cont)

38

An original story begins with an original idea. There's no one place to get ideas, but when you do get one, hold on to it.

Do you have any ideas?

Yes. The hero foolishly agrees to help a stooge write a story, only to find that the stooge has no ideas.

Okay. What happens next?

The stooge asks the hero what happens next.

Or you can put a fresh twist on an old idea. Either way, start by introducing the characters and setting up the situation.

Okay. A young couple, both of them are part Native American, buy their dream home ... only to find that it's built on a cursed racist-white-dude cemetery.

Were there racist-white-dude cemeteries?

In the 1800s, that's pretty much all there were.

The second part of a story is where you make the protagonists' plight worse. Try to do so in a unique and surprising way.

But the ghosts've had a century to see the error of their ways, so each night the couple is tormented by the heartfelt apologies of the dead!

OOH, YEAH! I'm picturing blood oozing out of the walls, spelling out the words "terribly sorry."

The last part is usually the protagonists getting out of trouble in a surprising way. The first thing they try should not work.

The couple brings in a medicine man.

And ...

The ghosts apologize even more profusely to him.

How will they ever get out of this?!

The three of them have to chant, "That's alright," one thousand times in Iroquois.

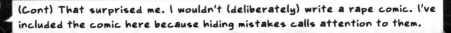

(Cont) That surprised me. I wouldn't (deliberately) write a rape comic. I've included the comic here because hiding mistakes calls attention to them.

39

When listing your top five films, number one should be easy. Pick the movie that's had the biggest impact on your life.

Number one's Raiders of the Lost Ark. It gave me my primary role model in life.

The Nazi who got his hand burned.

No, not him.

The Nazi who got caught in the propeller?

IT WASN'T A NAZI!

Well all the bald guys in that movie were Nazis!

Number two will be almost as easy. If you get stuck, think of what movie entertains you even after countless viewings.

So Belloq's your role model. Cool. What's your second favorite movie?

The Wrath of Khan.

Solid choice! What's your favorite part?

When the hero's best friend dies.

They resurrect him in the next movie.

Yeah, I didn't like that one quite as much.

Movies three through five can be tricky, but it's worth the effort. Making the list is fun, and telling patterns can emerge.

The Incredibles, The Empire Strikes Back, and The Army of Darkness.

Notice what your top five movies have in common?

They're all awesome?

None of them are targeted at adults.

Name one awesome thing that is.

Furthermore, your friends' reaction to your list, and the lists they create will tell you interesting things about them.

Three Minutes Later:

Those are my top five movies. They're all awesome, and they are all aimed at adults.

They're all "adult films."

Indeed. Are you denying that they are awesome?

I haven't seen the five you mentioned ...

But no. I don't deny their awesomeness.

Videotaping your will is a nice dramatic gesture. It gives you one last chance to communicate your feelings.

If you're seeing this, it means that I have died.

Or that my lawyer is showing this video to his friends as a goof.

Either way, I am not happy.

Don't waste this opportunity to tell the people in your life the things you've always wanted to say to them.

To my boss: I'd like to say that you are completely incompetent, both as a professional, and as a human being.

Man, it felt good to say that.

Which is why I said it every day, to anyone who'd listen.

Of course, the real business of a will is to give away stuff. Give your friends and family things they'll find meaningful.

My friend Rick shall receive the original source art for any comic I drew that insulted him.

The remaining 10% of my art will remain with my wife.

Try to leave some kind of lasting legacy. Something to make the world a better place for future generations.

Comics have been good to me. In an effort to give back, I shall fund a scholarship.

Every year it will go to the applicant who produces the best comic that insults Rick.

Also, some readers read this comic and thought I might be terminally ill. Some of you are thinking too much about this comic. More than I am, anyway.

"Riff" is a word comedians stole from jazz. It means to improvise and expand on an idea. First, you need an idea.

In judo, you use your opponent's own momentum against them, right?

Yeah.

Then couldn't you shut down a judo master by just not ever moving?

Hmmm. Victory through inaction.

It's the only kind of victory I know.

Now, explore the idea's ramifications. If something seems to disprove the idea, try to make it prove the idea instead.

Of course, you start each match by bowing.

Or do you? Maybe they just tell newbies that.

Oh, that's delightful! I bet every judo student's first real match ends with them flying through the air upside down thinking, "Note to self: never bow!"

Push the idea to illogical extremes. By now you'll be getting pretty silly. That's how you know you're doing it right.

When two judo masters fight, it looks like a staring contest. Neither one moves a muscle for hours until one of them makes a mistake.

What is that mistake?

He blinks.

Then, like lightning, the other judo master grabs him by the eyelids and flips him.

If you keep at it long enough the subject will naturally change itself, giving you new topics on which to "riff."

That's why there're no judo movies. It'd just be two guys doing nothing until the end of the movie.

There is one. "My Dinner With Andre."

In the end, Wallace Shawn grabs Andre by the eyelids and throws him across the restaurant.

WOW! I wish I'd stayed awake to see that!

I fell in love with this idea, but never thought anyone would like it. I also love Ric saying "that's delightful". He'd never say that. Nothing delights him.

12

People like to ask each other trivia questions, both for fun, and as a means of displaying their superior knowledge.

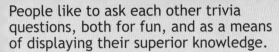

Get the terms of the question clearly defined. Nothing's worse than getting a question wrong on a technicality.

Relax and take your time answering the question. Answering right is far more important than answering quickly.

Know when to quit. It's pointless to suffer over something that's by definition trivial when the answer is available.

An idiot I know really did ask me this. He sat there like a jerk while I tried to answer, then admitted he didn't know the answer. This is a revenge comic.

First, let's be clear. By dreams I mean things your brain shows you while you're asleep, not things you hope will happen.

I had a dream last night.

I have a dream that you'll stop telling me about things I'm not interested in.

That's more of a goal.

A seemingly unattainable one.

When telling someone your dream, start by describing your dream's setting. This will give context to the dream's events.

I was watching TV, and Tim Gunn from Project Runway had a new show about a secret project he was working on.

Let me get this straight. You have dreams about watching TV?

My subconscious likes to keep it real.

Skip over the tedious details. The dream must have an interesting part. That's the only part you should be telling people.

Is there any aspect of this dream that makes it more interesting than a story about you watching TV?

Tim Gunn's secret project was that he was building a submarine.

Oh. That'll do.

Be aware that by telling people your dreams, you are leaving yourself wide open for their amateur psychoanalysis.

Clearly it's about your submerged wish to be homosexual, like Tim Gunn.

But there's much more to Tim Gunn than homosexuality!

Maybe I want to be thin, dignified, smart, successful, polite, and well dressed.

Yeah, doesn't disprove my theory.

I really did have this dream. To be honest, Tim spent most of the dream tidying up the build area. This dream means that DREAMS MEAN NOTHING!

Playing video games with someone else can be lots of fun. Many games are now made with "cooperative" play in mind.

I'm so glad we bought Rock Band: Hall and Oates!

I KNOW! It was frustrating at first, but once you get the hang of using the moustache, it rocks!

Even if a game was not designed for cooperative play, there are still ways to share the fun. Taking turns, for instance.

Okay, we switch in ten minutes, or when you get killed. Your turn starts ... NOW!

Cool.

BLAM

BDARG!

MY TURN!

Or one person can work the controls while the other acts as a spotter, looking for things the controller doesn't see.

There's a guy with a gun.

WHERE?!

BEHIND YOU!!

WHAT?!

ON THE SCREEN!!

THERE'S NO SCREEN BACK THERE!!

If you do use the pilot/navigator model, be sure each person on the team gets the job that best suits their abilities.

Look out for that truck. It'll kill you.

Okay.

Look out for that dog. It'll kill you.

Is there anything in this game that can't kill you?

Not that I've found. Look out for that shru

First, define the problem your invention will solve for your audience. This ensures that they'll understand the need.

People need a foolproof means of personal identification. High-tech retina scans are unreliable, and fingerprints are outdated.

DNA.

DNA takes too long.

Voice I.D. systems.

Uh, they have drawbacks.

Like the fact that you didn't know they exist?

Describe why your invention is uniquely able to solve the problem you described.

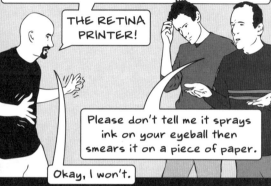

I'm working on an invention that combines the high-tech cachet of the retinal scan with the time-tested methods of finger printing.

THE RETINA PRINTER!

Please don't tell me it sprays ink on your eyeball then smears it on a piece of paper.

Okay, I won't.

Give people enough information that they'll know you aren't just making empty promises that you can't back up.

The eye has no ridges on it at all!

True.

Everyone's retina-print will look alike!

Yes, but each person's shriek of horror and discomfort is as unique as their fingerprint, and can be analyzed with off-the-shelf equipment.

Be aware that in today's world, just having a clever invention isn't enough. You also need a viable business model.

If you're just trying to cause people discomfort, why not jab them with a pin? It'd be simpler.

Yes, but then I couldn't sell my customers ink at an obscene mark-up.

I am horrified by your plan, and would like to invest.

The key to surviving the apocalypse is to have a plan. The simpler the plan is, the better its chances of success will be.

When society finally goes to $#!%, I'm gonna get a gun. Then I'm gonna find someone who's good at making plans, and I'll point the gun at them and make them make me a plan.

I can see a few problems with that plan.

Reeeeeally? ... Noted!

When that fateful day comes, you should immediately put your plan into effect. You can't hesitate, for others will not.

I take this to mean that society has gone to $#!%.

Yup. You work for me now.

I worked for you before. The total collapse of modern civilization doesn't seem to change my lifestyle at all.

That's funny!

No, it isn't.

Don't be too dogmatic about sticking to the plan. You have to allow yourself to improvise from time to time.

Well, as your planner, I think your first move should be to give me the gun.

Nah. %$#*!!

That said, it is vital that you stick to the plan. After all, it's gotten you this far.

Five Years Later:

A newcomer has arrived. He's healthy, and genetically viable. What should I do?

Give me the gun.

We've been over that.

Very well. Destroy the newcomer.

BRAINO HAS SPOKEN! DEATH TO THE NEWCOMER!

And stop calling me "Braino."

We've been over that, too.

If society fell, I wouldn't be the planner. I'd be the guy in the torn tuxedo who announces the warlord's entrance. I'm really good at yelling "Behold".

Even if your current operating system is working for you, there are many good reasons to upgrade your computer.

There are many ways to upgrade your operating system, each with its own benefits and costs. Choose carefully.

Before starting, back up all of your data, and gather the installation disks for all of your programs and applications.

Upgrading can be nerve-wracking and difficult, but the results outlast the pain.

How to Save Money

Even if you keep a tight rein on your money already, there're almost certainly places where you're overspending.

How was the movie?

They wanted $7.50 for a large drink!

So I assume you got a small drink.

No way! The small costs $7.00! If I'm gonna get ripped off, it's gonna be for something big.

It disturbs me that that seems logical.

Once you've identified such an area, find an alternative that will give you the same benefit at a lower cost.

Next time I'm gonna buy a great big drink at 7-11 and smuggle it in under my hat, like Abe Lincoln used to. Of course, he didn't have a 7-11 to buy drinks at, but still.

That's why Booth shot him. Booth was an actor, and they were paid out of the concession stand's profits. Isn't history fascinating?

Yes, when you tell it.

Don't be afraid to make refinements to the plan as needed. Even the best plans may need some tinkering.

I could just smuggle cans of pop in my pants!

Aren't you worried about getting caught?

I'm more worried about the cans getting warm.

And parts of me getting cold.

Parts near PLEASE STOP!!

You're right. There may be theater employees near.

Know when to stop tinkering. Destroying the benefit of the thing you're spending on to save a few cents is pointless.

I realized I could save even more money if I made my own soft drinks! Care for some bathtub Mountain Dew?

That sounds really dirty.

I rinsed the tub.

That does not help.

Panel two was just a chance to work out my Hodgman envy. Also, I had trouble deciding between "Bathtub Mountain Dew" and "Bathtub Mr. Pibb."

The most heartless weapons designer of all time was Mother Nature. Use the natural world for inspiration.

Gentlemen, what's the most dangerous animal?

A shark!

No.

A bear?

No.

You with an idea?

No.

Shut up.

If your design is truly advanced, you'll have to convince people of its worth.

The answer, of course, is an elephant with a gun.

Technically, it'd be the gun that's dangerous.

Guns don't kill people. Elephants with guns kill people.

Can't argue with that.

Not without losing some dignity.

Don't focus solely on offensive weapons. Defense is equally important. A weapon is useless if it has been destroyed.

Here it is! A mechanical elephant with guns for tusks. It's 50 feet tall and covered with armor everywhere ... except on the bottom.

You do realize you've created a weapons platform that's vulnerable to tripping?

IMPOSSIBLE!

Unless they use a rope.

At the end of the day, a weapon is just a tool, and is useless unless it is wielded as part of an intelligent strategy.

It's invulnerable, so long as the rebels don't shoot up at it, or own a rope. We'll paint it and our soldiers' armor white, while we wear dark colors. That way all the fire will be drawn away from us.

Unless there's a battle in some snowy environment.

What are the odds of that?

Actually, the most dangerous animal is the Hippo, and in the prequels, the walkers are more hippo like. Who says the prequels weren't an improvement?

It's easy and tempting to vilify your enemies, but if you examine them, they may not be all that different from you.

> It occurs to me, Rocket Hat, that you and I are not so different.

> We're both virile, manly he-men.

> We're both most at home in the sky. (The moon is in the sky, after all.)

> We both long for the warm embrace of your girlfriend.

This insight can be useful, as knowledge of yourself can then be used as a weapon against your adversary.

> And, neither of us is really much of a threat when we're encased up to the navel in moon-concrete!

> Please don't ask me how I found this fact out.

Be aware that understanding may lead to sympathy, making you reluctant to take action against your foe.

> In a different life, we might have been friends. It's a shame I have to kill you.

> There are alternatives, Sire.

> True! On second thought, it's a shame I have to have my moon-men kill you while I cower safely in another room, far, far away.

> That is a shame.

Also, guard against complacency. If your enemy is worthy of you they will still find ways to surprise you.

> Rocket Hat attacked his guards and escaped, Sire!

> BUT HOW?! His limbs were immobilized! How could he attack anyone?

> Rocket-propelled head-butt.

> NGAAAAH! OUCH! His hat's so pointy!

> And now we know why.

> I hate to pat myself on the back, but "we both long for the warm embrace of your girlfriend" is one of my favorite things I've ever written.

How to Create a Commercially Viable Series of Popular Books

When making a calculated attempt to sell books at all costs, planning is key. Start by picking your target audience.

> I've decided to start writing children's books.

> You hate children.

> And books.

> Yes, but I like money, and kids' books are a big business.

> Doing things you hate for people you hate to make money. I can relate to that ... boss.

Then, develop an original concept with obvious commercial appeal. It should seem novel, but have almost no risk.

> My plan is to take books that were popular with adults, and adapt them for the children's market.

> So, your "idea" is to take other people's ideas and profit from them.

> Yup! What do you think?

> Eh, it's been done.

Now, write something. The best concept on Earth is worthless until it takes the form of a finished manuscript.

FUN AND LAUGHING IN LAS VEGAS

> HAW HAW!

> HEE!

We were somewhere around Barstow on the edge of the desert when we got the giggles.

When marketing your books, look to other, similar projects to gauge your chances of success in the marketplace.

> I just don't think kids'll buy this. How would you feel if someone took a kids' story and tried to sell it to you as an adult?

> Name three movies that came out in the last year.

> "G.I. Joe," "Land of the Lost," "Where the Wild Things Are."

> I'll shut up now.

For more on this idea, please go to page 139. If you haven't read or seen "Fear and Loathing in Las Vegas", do that first.

How to Express Gratitude for an Unexpected Gift (Based on a True Story)

When someone surprises you, it can be hard to know how to react.

I've got something for you.

BAGH! DON'T HIT ME!

It's a computer. I built it for you. It's out in my truck.

Wha ... WOW! That's great!

And I'm gonna hit you with it.

BDGAAGH!

Just kidding.

Try to find out if there is a specific reason for the gift.

I don't get it. Why'd you do this?

Because you're my brother.

And?

I had the parts laying around.

And?

And that weak-@$$ piece of crud you've been calling your computer is an insult to the Meyer name.

Now I get it.

In any case, don't over-thank the gift giver. Gushing with gratitude is irritating at best, and often seems insincere.

Thanks, man.

Don't mention it.

I appreciate it.

It's no big deal.

This is so nice of you.

Really you're doing me a favor. You're taking my refuse.

In that case, you're welcome.

That's very gracious of you.

The best way to thank someone for generosity is to be generous yourself.

Well, the least I can do is put you in a comic.

You don't have to do that.

And I'll depict you as taller and thinner than me, with much more hair.

Well thanks.

Believe me, it's my pleasure.

True story. My brother saw my computer and was unimpressed. He built me a better computer out of spare parts. I gave him a ridiculous moustache.

53

The Halloween costume industry may seem random and disorganized, but it follows patterns, just like any other.

> I've noticed that women's Halloween costumes are getting sexier.

> And I'm in favor of it.

> As are we all. But I've noticed that men's costumes aren't getting sexier at all.

> Again, I'm in favor of it.

> Again, as are we all.

Based on your knowledge of the past, use your imagination and intuition to try to predict the industry's future trends.

> But think about it. Take Batman; what would a "sexy Batman" costume be?

> Deeply disturbing.

> Yes, but what would it be made up of?

> A mask, a cape, and a Speedo.

> Exactly!

> With a bat on the Speedo for the "deluxe package."

Once you've predicted a trend, develop a business model to capitalize on your knowledge of the industry's direction.

> Now tell me. What would be a "Sexy Dracula" costume?

> Fangs, a Speedo, and a cape.

> "Sexy Darth Vader?"

> It's the same thing! You could just crank out cheap capes and swimsuits and make a mint by changing out the masks!

> The only challenge would be looking at yourself in the mirror.

> But you could afford a really nice mirror.

All that's left now is to execute your plan and if you were correct, you'll see your finances and your reputation improve.

Fifty Years Later:

> These two men did more to make Halloween creepy and disturbing than anyone since Edgar Allan Poe.

> You may recognize them. To this day, two of the most popular men's costumes are meant to be likenesses of them.

> As you well know, the costumes consist of rubber masks, Speedos, and capes.

People never want to be boring. If someone bores you, often a subtle hint will be enough to make them stop.

I was so bored this weekend.

Aww, I hate to hear that.

All weekend, nothing but boredom.

I hate to hear that.

Um, you're repeating yourself.

And yet I'm still hearing "that."

If subtlety doesn't stop the boring story, try making your hints increasingly obvious and hard to ignore.

I was just sooooooo bored.

You've painted me a vivid word-picture of your appalling boredom.

Bored, bored, booooooored.

It's as if I'm there, bored with you.

I've never been that bored.

Neither had I, until now!

If you can't stop the story, and you can't remove yourself from the situation, try to find some entertainment in it.

I was so bored I started counting the beer commercials. You ever been so bored you started counting stupid things?

Seventy-seven.

Seventy-eight.

Like maybe the number of times someone says the word bored?

Yeah, like that.

Yes I have.

The most important thing is to remember the experience and try not to bore people yourself in the future.

She was telling a boring story about being bored! It was boredom squared!

And now you're telling me about it.

But this is an interesting story.

Because?

I was so incredibly bored.

I hate to hear that.

Someone bored me. I told my wife, boring her. She pointed it out, so I wrote this comic. Now you can bore people by telling them about this comic.

First, find something you enjoy, but which other people do not get at all.

Have you ever seen the show "The Prisoner"?

No.

It was great!

It was about this guy ...

This guy who was a prisoner.

I kinda figured.

Try to interest those around you in whatever it is. It's a sneaky way to identify those who aren't "into it."

So, who's holding him?

Dunno.

Where's he being held?

Dunno.

Do you know his name?

Nope.

Have YOU ever seen the show "The Prisoner"?!

Find someone who shares your interest and talk about it loudly and endlessly, when nobody else within earshot cares.

I liked the one where they hypnotized him to believe that he was left-handed.

Or the one where he ran for president of the prison!

I liked the episode where they explained everything so it all made perfect sense.

There's no episode like that.

Oh. Then I don't like any episode.

If what you're enjoying is truly good, the world will catch on. When it does, you can act superior to the newcomers.

That remake of "The Prisoner" AMC is making looks pretty good!

Hopefully it'll make sense this time.

You just don't understand "The Prisoner."

Nobody does!

Exactly!!

The title of this one is a reference to "Fear and Loathing in Las Vegas." Also, the remake of "The Prisoner" did make more sense, and was not good.

Be considerate. Lack of consideration is the root of all rudeness. Consideration for others is the definition of class.

A class act knows that anything worth doing is worth doing right. Attention to detail is the hallmark of class.

On a related note, having class means knowing quality when you see it, and insisting on the best when it's available.

Squandering money is never classy, but neither is penny-pinching. Don't be afraid to spend money when necessary.

No-win situations usually start out looking innocent, or else nobody would ever get trapped by them.

Someone needs to tell Jenkins to fill out his RJ-17 form.

You are someone.

Are you trying to tell me something?

Yes.

Why not make someone else tell me? That seems to be your go-to move.

Often, by the time you realize you're in trouble, it's too late to get out of it.

You need to fill out your RJ-17 form.

Not gonna happen.

Then please tell the boss that I told you to.

Why would I do that?

If you don't, it'll make me look bad.

Never mind.

If you think you're trapped in a no-win situation, analyze the situation carefully, looking for the least damaging outcome.

If I say I told him and he says I didn't, I look like a liar.

If I say I told him and he refused, I look ineffectual.

Keep complaining about it and you'll look like a whiner.

But an honest, effective whiner.

Even the most hopeless situations can be defeated if you think creatively, and have the fortitude to act on your ideas.

You told me to talk to Jenkins? I won't do it.

You get to tell accounting.

Tell them what? That you tried to get me to do your job for you, or that I refused?

Tell them they don't need to send you a paycheck any more.

Never mind.

 Wow. Re-reading this one, it strikes me that I lose in every panel.

When giving someone a gift you know is bad, try to manage their expectations.

It's a snow globe!

Why'd you cross out all the E's?

Open the box and find out!

To some extent.

Once the bad gift has been revealed, frame the debate in a flattering light. Describe the gift's negatives as positives.

It's all melted.

Not "melted," "Customized!" No other wife on Earth will get a "Snow Glob" like this for Christmas.

That's probably true.

You might have to approach your positive spin campaign from several angles before you find one that works.

The snow's all melted into a big gray clump.

The little Santa and the village in there are melted and charred.

Imagine he's a mutant in a post apocalyptic war zone.

I'm gonna be using my imagination an awful lot.

Imagine it's a meteor.

Think of it as an exercycle for your right brain.

It feels bad, giving someone a terrible gift, then tricking them into being happy, but if they're happy, does it matter?

I see you're enjoying your "Snow Glob"!

I'm pretending the mutant is you.

Glad that increased imagination is paying off.

I'm trying to hit the mutant with the meteor.

Actually, it takes very little imagination at all.

Some ideas come to me so fully formed that I worry I might be plagiarizing something. I misspelled "Snow Globe" and five minutes later I'd written this.

How to Tell Someone That They Are Wrong (Based on a real idiotic conversation)

There are matters of opinion and taste that can be argued, but most people agree, some things are just wrong.

> I rented that new Star Trek movie.

> I didn't like it.

> YOU ARE WRONG!!

If you are to consider yourself an open-minded person, you have to try to see the issue from your adversary's side.

> I didn't like the ending.

> Well, I can see that.

> I was also disappointed ...

> That it ended.

If you can't see any reason for your adversary's position, ask them. They may have a point that didn't occur to you.

> I mean, they just get back on the ship and go back out into space for another adventure.

> What kinda ending is that?

> The kind of ending they used for every Star Trek movie.

> And episode.

> Ever.

Once you understand their idea, explain logically why they're wrong. They should see reason, unless they are a monster.

> Look, does that mean you don't like James Bond movies because he stays with British Intelligence and will get another assignment?

> Actually, I don't like Bond movies.

> YOU'RE A MONSTER!

The guy this is about openly admits to his part of the conversation. He's PROUD of it! When this comic made the front page of Digg, he took credit.

Proposing marriage is one of the most nerve-wracking things a man will ever do. Most men seek out advice first.

I'm planning to ask my girlfriend to marry me.

Good for you!

I want it to be memorable.

It will be. Women never forget the day they turn down and humiliate a guy.

The person asking might want your ideas, but more often they will want your opinion of ideas they already have.

I heard about a guy who set up a scavenger hunt for his girlfriend, and the last item was the ring.

Is that romantic?

Oh yeah! Scavenger hunts are the most romantic of the elementary school group activities.

If they do present an idea, express your opinions honestly, and give thought-out reasons why you approve or disapprove.

The more I think about it, the more I like the scavenger hunt idea.

I'm glad you approve.

Why ask her if she's willing to marry you when you can make her prove she's worthy of you with a test of her intelligence!

Once they have settled on a plan, try to help them expand on it to make it more unique and personal.

You could write a romantic word search puzzle and give it to her.

A romantic word search?

Yeah, make it heart-shaped or something.

You're just messing with me, aren't you?

You could write "marry me" on a Rubik's Cube, then scramble it!

First, invent a hero who has a unique power they can use to fight crime.

What's your plan, Omnipresent Man?

Since I'm everywhere at once, I can easily infiltrate the criminal gang and tell you their plans.

Is that admissible as evidence?

Dunno. I'm not a law-expert.

Lawyer.

Whatever.

Waste no time in introducing the villains over which your hero is sure to prevail.

Meanwhile, at the criminal hide-out:

You're gonna rat on us, Omnipresent Man!

How'd you know?!?

You said it just now. I think you were talking to a cop somewhere.

I was lying. I've gone bad. How dare you listen to my private conversations? Who do you think you are?

A criminal who was standing right here.

Life for a hero isn't easy. They often have friction with their allies as well as from their numerous enemies.

Meanwhile, at the police station:

So, you've gone bad!

You said it just now.

What makes you think that?!

I was lying! It's part of the gig! I lie to you, to criminals, to my wife! I have to lie to serve the greater good!

Are you sure you're not a lawyer?

If your superhero is to be relatable as a character, they should have problems in their personal life as well.

Meanwhile, at Omnipresent Man's home:

What do you lie to me about?

OH FOR $#@$'s SAKE!

You'd better get yourself a law-expert.

Turns out they're called lawyers.

I know.

I'm often asked why Omnipresent Man only shows up once in each frame. He can choose when and how he's visible ... I guess.

It's one of the less pleasant aspects of the human condition, but most people are put off by people who are too happy.

Rick, you're happy!

Yes, I'm happy.

Why?

What? Can't a man be happy?

A MAN can, but we're talking about you here.

Despite any feelings of discomfort you may experience, you should try to ferret out the source of their happiness.

I'm in love.

Good! I hope you and your newest crazy woman will be very happy.

I'm not dating a crazy woman.

Fine. "Crazy man." Whatever you're into.

Once you've found the reason, don't over-analyze it. To do so risks destroying the happiness, which would be cruel.

So you're saying only a crazy woman would be attracted to me?

No, I'm saying only crazy women ever get into relationships with you.

Whether they start mentally ill, or the experience of being courted by you drives them insane is open for debate.

Don't worry though. If they're truly happy it will be exceedingly difficult to destroy their good mood.

Psychiatrists use an inkblot that looks like you to diagnose female patients.

Just one psychiatrist, and she's my ex-wife, so she doesn't really count.

How's she doing, by the way?

She's good. She had a puppet of me made!

Sweet!

Panel three dates back to conversations Ric and I had ten years ago. Back then it wasn't dating Ric we thought made you crazy, but living in Montana.

The following are suggestions to help you grow up. If you think it'll happen on its own, you're confusing it with getting old.

One important step on the road to adulthood is to recognize that most of your problems are self-inflicted.

Another step on the path to maturity is to realize that your parents were no smarter or more perfect than you are.

By the same token, recognize that your heroes, much like your parents, are just as fallible and flawed as anyone else.

 That Johnny Paycheck album also featured a "funny" song about killing a narc, and a song with the line "you shed no tear when he stretched my ear."

Many adult males spend a surprising amount of time and effort trying to appear as if they are "manly."

Nothing says "I'm a man" quite like a moustache.

I would hope your genitalia would send a pretty clear message.

But I can't show that to people the first time we meet.

You know that from experience, don't you?

If you must deliberately make a show of your "manliness," think about "manly men" and emulate their behavior.

Lots of guys in the really manly jobs tend to have moustaches.

Cowboys. Cops.

Construction workers. Bikers.

Exactly.

Come to think of it, all of the Village People had moustaches except the Native American.

When choosing your role models, be clear on what aspects of the male character you value as being "manly."

The Village People aren't really the example of manhood I was looking for.

Well, they were talented, they knew who they were, and they weren't afraid to put it out there for all to see.

But they weren't really "men's men."

That depends on what you mean by "men's men."

Don't sweat it, though. Nothing is less "manly" than sitting around worrying about whether you're "manly" enough.

I was thinking of someone like Clint Eastwood.

He never had a moustache. But lots of the guys he shot in the Dirty Harry movies did.

And nothing's manlier than getting shot by Dirty Harry.

True, he didn't shoot women. Often.

I was going to say that John Wayne didn't worry about seeming manly. Then I realized that he must have or he wouldn't've changed his name from Marion.

If someone asks what "the hell" you're doing, it's often because they know what you're doing, but don't want to face it.

What the hell are you doing?

I've made myself into a masking tape mummy!

You say that like it's the most obvious thing in the world.

Well, look at me.

Okay, point taken.

Often the issue is not that they don't get what you're doing, but that they can't understand why you're doing it.

What a waste of time. And tape.

Bertrand Russell said, "Time you enjoy wasting isn't wasted."

And the same goes for masking tape?

No, the tape's wasted, but I stole it from work.

Don't get defensive. Just calmly explain why what you're doing is a good idea, or at least not as bad an idea as they think.

It's not going to be fun taking all that tape off.

Au contraire! I've avoided all of my hairier regions, and soon my clothes will be lint free!

Very nice! This is the smartest stupid thing you have ever done.

You may never get people to understand your actions, but you might get them to accept your actions, which is something.

You're a silly, silly man.

Careful. Make me angry and you face the curse of the masking tape mummy.

And that would be?

The masking tape mummy standing here cursing.

I can live with that. $%‡@!

I LOVE the show "Phineas and Ferb." I wrote this comic, then, much later, saw an episode where Ferb holds a blueprint that says "Masking Tape Mummy Gymnastics." This is either a coincidence, an homage or accidental plagiarism. I'll let you decide.

If you're going to kill off a fictional character, you should first devise a believable source of deadly peril.

> Pitiful Earth-Men! As a gift, we Moon-Men are sending you a sample of Moon-Technology. It is a device with a thousand and one peaceful uses.

> It is called the Slaughter-Bot.

> When it arrives, I suggest you gather in large, unarmed groups to gawk at it.

> It is really cool looking.

Then, come up with a reason for many of your characters to be together in one place, so that all of them are at risk.

> He was right. It is cool looking.

> Especially the awesome way it's exploding as Rocket-Hat is effortlessly destroying it.

> And the way the firelight is glinting off of the shrapnel, which is headed right at us.

Choose carefully. A key character's loss will shock your audience. The death of a side character will be seen as a cop-out.

> RODNEY'S BEEN HIT!

> Rodney. My mechanic. The guy on the ground.

> Who?

> Oh.

> Poor, poor Rodney. We hardly knew ye.

> Too true.

Once they are dead, keep them dead. Resurrecting them will make the whole thing seem like a cheap marketing ploy.

> I'm okay! The shrapnel hit my spare copy of "Help Is on the Way: A Collection of Basic Instructions." Owning it saved my life!

> Thank God you're alive! Now you can explain to me who the #$!! you are.

Rodney's a real guy as well. He's a stand-up comic. Go see him if you get the chance. www.rodneysherwood.com!

Unless your friends are exact clones of you, they will be interested in things that do not interest you.

Don't get it.
I wake up early.
Got it.
Every day.
Got it.
And I run three miles.
Got it.
For fun.
I don't get it.

Having a friend love something that's of no interest to you is a fine opportunity to learn more about that thing.

I did enjoy watching you in that freaky runners' parade that one time.
It's called a marathon.
It's your scene, man. Call it whatever you like.

If their interest is truly alien to you, there's entertainment value in examining their hobby in an effort to understand.

Even if you didn't understand it, I'm glad you enjoyed the marathon.
It was all healthy, athletic people looking miserable. What's not to enjoy?

At the very least, a passing knowledge of their interests will give you gift ideas.

Did you get that MP3 I sent you of the best running song ever recorded by man?
Yakety Sax?
Benny Hill could really haul ass!

If marathon organizers were serious about drawing a crowd, you'd get time deducted from your overall score for wearing something embarrasing.

A good photograph seldom happens on its own. A well-composed photo will take a great deal of effort and thought.

If you're stuck for ideas, there are many "stock poses" that everyone has seen. These can serve as a good starting point.

Don't be a perfectionist. Overanalyzing and fussing over your subject can lead to a photo that's lifeless or awkward.

Often an action shot, though less slick and polished, will have more soul and capture your subject more fully.

 In every picture of me as a kid, I'm grimacing. Part because my "toothy" smile looks weird. Part because Mom was always yelling "NO! SMILE PRETTY!"

Panel 1:

If you are involved in anything creative, and have friends, eventually your friends will have a few ideas for you.

Did you like that idea I sent you for your comic?

The superhero based on you, that fights crime with knives?

That's right, "The Knifeketeer"!

Before I answer, tell me this ...

Do you have any knives on you now?

Panel 2:

If their idea is good and will work, go with it. If the idea is flawed and unworkable, tell them diplomatically.

I just don't think a super hero should stab people.

Tell that to Wolverine.

No, for two reasons. He doesn't exist, and if he did, he'd stab me.

Panel 3:

Don't be dismissive. Give your friend a chance to fix the idea. You might get a usable idea, or at least not lose a friend.

He doesn't have to kill people.

So he heroically wounds people?

He doesn't have to hurt anyone! Green Arrow had non-lethal arrows.

They were arrows tipped with big green boxing gloves.

You can come up with something better if you put some effort into it.

That's a big "if."

Panel 4:

Even if you have to change their idea substantially, it may pan out to be great.

I threatened to punch the mugger with my fist-knife and he stopped resisting.

Yes, because he was laughing too hard to breathe. That's another criminal caught by "The Human Joke"!

Um, I call myself "The Knifeketeer"!

Yeah, I know.

 The real Ric did suggest the Knifeketeer as a superhero for himself to portray. The respect he gets, and the boxing glove knife were my ideas.

When facing a task that you're dreading, don't ignore it. It will not go away. Only by assessing it honestly can you prepare.

Avoid negativity. Life's hard enough without everyone telling you how hard it is. Talk to people with a positive outlook.

Rather than focusing on how difficult or unpleasant your task will be, try to view it as an interesting challenge.

While engaged in the task, stay focused on the positive. It can't last forever, and you may surprise yourself by enjoying it.

Everybody makes mistakes. The measure of a person is how well he or she deals with the mistakes they have made.

> We're sending a marked-up copy of your second book for you to correct. Amazingly, you made all the same mistakes you made on the first book.

> Oh well. Consistency is a virtue.

> Yeah, not when you're consistently wrong.

Ignoring mistakes won't make them disappear. It's much better to face them honestly, and with a sense of humor.

> The edits for my second book came.

> Why's it so big? The book's only 100 pages.

> There were so many errors they did three printings. One for spelling, one for grammar, and one for wordiness.

> Is that one just printed in red ink?

> On red paper.

If you honestly don't feel you've made a mistake, defend your actions and try to convince others that you are right.

> That character's meant to be plain-spoken and folksy. The "errors" in his dialog are deliberate.

> I think a farmer would know how to pronounce the word "farm."

> Listen, city boy, I grew up on a fram, and I know how framers talk.

In the end, the only mature way to deal with a mistake is to admit it, correct it, and learn from it.

> Well, I hope you've learned your lesson.

> Yes. Next book I'll set aside more time to make corrections.

> Or, you could try to make fewer mistakes in the first place.

> HA! Now who hasn't learned their lesson?

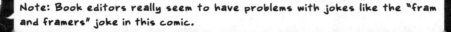

Note: Book editors really seem to have problems with jokes like the "fram and framers" joke in this comic.

How to Use the Various Shades and Styles of Sarcasm

Sarcasm takes many forms. One of the most common is to strongly agree with a bad idea, for an insulting reason.

> I'm thinking of getting my baby's ears pierced. I figure now is the perfect time.

> Agreed. If your baby is ugly, you have to start dressing them up as early as possible!

One sarcasm delivery vector is the false misunderstanding. It makes the victim feel foolish, and expresses your opinion.

> My baby isn't ugly. I just figure if I get her ears pierced now, she won't complain when it hurts. She'll just cry, and she does that anyway. Also, I'll get to pick out the earrings, not her!

> Oh. Sorry. I thought that when you as her mother said it was the perfect time, you meant it was the perfect time for her, not you. Silly of me.

Another mode of sarcasm is to push the victim's logic to its illogical conclusion.

> That's a logical plan.

> Thanks.

> While you're at it, you should get her a tattoo.

> What?!

> Yeah, get her an itty-bitty tramp stamp now. It'll be tiny and cost almost nothing, but it'll grow with her and by time she's 16, it'll look huge and expensive!

These are a few techniques. Mastering them all will make you more likely to see when they're being used against you.

> She liked the idea.

> You mean she showed questionable judgement? SHOCKING!

> Well, on the bright side, no reputable tattoo artist would tattoo a baby.

> Yes, and she'd only go to the most reputable artist available.

Hyperbole is intentional, bombastic exaggeration. It is a powerful oratory technique that is easy to misuse.

I AM THE GREATEST AT HYPERBOLE. Nobody hyperbolizes with more ...

Um ...

Hyperbolity.

Uh, yeah, that'll do.

The whole point of hyperbole is to go big. Tepid hyperbole isn't hyperbole at all, just lame exaggeration or bragging.

Well, don't underestimate my levels of hyperbolity. I can be quite hyperbolic when I'm in the mood.

AND I AM IN THE MOOD ...

Surprisingly often.

You can only engage in hyperbole for so long until you'll be expected to prove one of your overblown claims.

You know nothing of the hyperbolistic arts! You can't even spell hyperbole.

Oh, I can spell hyperbole. I can spell the crap out of it.

I just don't wanna.

It's true that using hyperbole puts you at a certain risk, but if others retaliate with hyperbole, they assume the same risk.

This is the dumbest conversation you two have ever had.

Dumber than the one about what superhero would win a slap fight?

Yes.

Or who'd win a slap war between all of the superheroes?

Yes.

Is it dumber than this conversation we're having with you right now?

Uh ... oh dear.

Forgive me if this is obvious, but many don't seem to realize that to be the life of the party, you must attend parties.

I heard you were throwing a party.

Did you hear that you weren't invited?

Yup.

Well, come in. You do realize that it's BYOB?

That must have been written on the invitation you didn't send me.

To be the life of the party you must bring something unique. Some skill you possess that can "liven up" said party.

I brought my guitar!

I don't know. Everyone seems to be enjoying just talking to each other.

Don't worry about that.

They'll all shut up when I start playing.

They wont want to be rude.

No. They won't.

Choose your moment. If there's a lull in conversation, or if someone expresses an interest in your skill, spring into action.

Play us a song, you're the piano maaaaaaaaan! Play us a soooong toniiiiiiiiight! We're all in the mood for a melody, and you've got us feelin' all riiiiiiiiiiiiiiiiiiiiiiiiiiiiiiiiiiiiiiiiiiiiiiiiiiiiiiiiight!

That was... something.

Glad you liked it. I'll play it again.

It's fiiiiiiiiiiiiiiiiiiive o'clock on a Saturdaaaaay.

Watch your fellow partygoers. Figure out what they want and give them that. The whole idea is for everyone to have fun.

Any requests?

Do you know "While My Guitar Gently Weeps"?

Only on the trombone.

Oh! That's a pity!

I've got it out in the car!

Oh. That IS a pity.

To play a guitar at a party is to say "Shut up and pay attention to me." It's irritating, and it usually interrupts the argument I'm having about Star Trek.

Powerful superhero teams are usually drawn together by either a unique challenge or a supernatural being.

For eons I've observed the actions of man. His plans. His schemes. His petty failures and his massive failures.

I am known as The Judger, and I am not impressed.

The heroes in a team must be chosen carefully so that their strengths and abilities will complement each other.

Rocket Hat, Omnipresent Man, and the Human Joke.

Pardon me ...

A.K.A. the Knifeketeer.

Thank you.

I gathered you because you'll be easier for me to observe if you're all in one place.

That's pretty lazy.

Don't judge. That's my job.

Once your team is assembled, some members will naturally stand out as obvious leaders.

Rocket Hat is right. We need to organize to be an effective force for good!

Rocket Hat's also correct that we'll need a bold leader!

Will you see fit to lead them, Rocket Hat?

Silence implies consent. It is decided.

Of course, any time a group of heroes forms, an equally impressive group of villains will form to challenge them.

None can withstand the might of the Moon-Men and the ... foul-mouthed spaghetti monster.

It's *%$# masking tape. And I curse 'cause I'm a %$e#ing mummy

Whatever. The details...

Let me guess, THE DETAILS ARE UN-IMPORTANT!!

GET OUTTA HERE, OMNIPRESENT MAN!

I am "out of here." SHUT UP!!!

I meant for the masking tape to look like the thin kind. Many readers said it looked like spaghetti. I widened it for the cover of this book.

Sometimes, if you're lucky, you'll derive a surprising amount of satisfaction from something remarkably trivial.

I got a really great shave this morning!

No cuts, no irritation, and all the hair is gone.

So, it's great in that you did a good job without injuring yourself.

For me, that's a big deal.

Don't be self conscious. Life is too short to let feeling silly rob you of happiness.

HMMMM. Ooooh. Ahhhhhh.

Is there a reason that you're rubbing your face and making happy noises?

Yes.

Good.

I guess.

Indeed, rather than hiding your joy, you should share it with others. Tell people why you're happy. Maybe it will spread.

I shaved well this morning, my friend. It's so smoooooth. You wanna feel the smooooothness?

No.

You don't know what you're missing.

Smooooothness?

Okay, maybe you do know.

Allowing yourself to enjoy the little things will often have a positive cumulative effect on your entire day.

Did you spend all day at work rubbing your face and moaning?

Yes.

And how'd your coworkers react to that?

By shunning me but good!

And what did that teach you?

That I can avoid conversations by rubbing my face and moaning.

That's not what HMMMM. Ooooh. Ahhhhhh.

Sometimes people will offer you a food item you do not like and it falls to you to politely decline.

You want an apple? I got a bunch of Red Deliciouses on my desk.

Red Delicious apples. The crappy fruit whose name is a lie.

Go get one.

Yeah, no thanks.

Make sure the person offering the food understands that it's the food you are rejecting, not them or their hospitality.

You don't want my apples? You should at least taste my apples. My apples are sweet, and so very full of juice.

Ugh. No thanks.

Afraid of getting sticky?

I just don't like Red Delicious apples, okay?

So you'd eat something else if I offered it?

I'll take that on a case-by-case basis.

They may think you're refusing the food in an attempt to be polite. Give reasons you don't like the food item in question.

I grew up in the area where they grow Red Delicious apples, and being constantly surrounded by them made me hate them.

:CRUNCH:

Same goes for country music.

:CRUNCH:

And dudes with mullets.

:CRUNCH:

I'm sorry, I couldn't hear over my apple. What'd you say?

Nothing.

They'll try to use logic or even guilt to make you eat whatever it is. Stand firm. Eating something you hate helps no one.

You liked that apple pie Kate brought in.

Apples were just one ingredient. It had butter in it too, that doesn't mean I like to just eat me a big stick of Land-O-Lakes.

But I've seen you

All right, butter was a bad example.

I grew up in apple country, and hate Red Delicious apples. I also don't drink milk. I grew up near a dairy, and I know they squeeze it out of cows.

When making a purchase, it's tempting to buy the cheapest or fanciest item, but I suggest buying the highest quality item.

Look what I just bought! It's the world's most accurate ruler!

Can it measure my disapproval?

In metric, all the way up to 10,000 milliscorns!

Quality items are usually more durable than cheap items, making the extra cost an investment that pays off over time.

It's milled from solid stainless steel. It won't ever stain, even if you get blood on it.

How would you... let me rephrase that. How DID you get blood on a ruler?

Accidentally. The edges are sharp.

A quality item usually does its job better than a cheap item, or a needlessly fancy item that's meant primarily for looks.

This so-called eight and a half by eleven paper is three sixteenths of an inch short!

I'd always suspected.

No, wait. I was holding the ruler crooked. Heh, I'm not qualified to use a ruler.

I'd always suspected.

It takes willpower to buy the best, not the cheapest or fanciest, but your sense of satisfaction will be worth the effort.

Now to put it with my space-pen and the fifty-sheet stapler.

In the junk drawer.

The world's greatest junk drawer.

Why do you need all these desk accessories? You do everything on your computer.

You're right! I should buy the world's best computer next.

If you do, make sure it's stainless steel, 'cause there will be blood.

A presentation has three parts. An intro, a body, and a conclusion. In the intro you tell them what you're going to tell them.

The middle part of a presentation is called the body. This is where you tell the audience what you're telling them.

A presentation ends with the conclusion, which is your last chance to sum up the information you're trying to convey.

Structure may seem detrimental to your creativity, but it adds clarity to your presentation, and that's a good thing.

 I shouldn't pick on public schools. I attended public school, and I learned there that a presentation has three parts ...

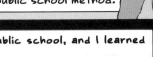

Strange as it seems, the easy part of innovating is to get an idea. Everyone has ideas. Execution is the hard part.

> I've got an idea.

> Seeing you getting excited about an idea is like finding a warm spot in a swimming pool. It feels good, but it makes me kinda uneasy.

> Now I have two ideas. One of them is to pee on you.

Once you've settled on your idea, embellish it. Work out the details and determine if the idea is feasible.

> People love French fries. People love ice cream.

> And you thought, "I'll combine them, and ruin them both."

> I call it "French friescream"!

> Great name. It combines french fries and screaming.

Now drill down into the specifics. Focus on what you will have to do to make your idea into a reality.

> So, you're thinking, what, potato-flavored ice cream with crispy hunks of fried batter?

> That's one option.

> Or are you just thinking this'll be a way to sell frozen mashed potatoes at an obscene markup?

> That is another option.

Discuss your idea with others. Their insights may help shape your idea, or tell you if the idea's worth pursuing at all.

> What do you think? Your opinion is important to me.

> I think it's a good idea. So, what's the next step?

> Coming up with another idea.

> You said my opinion was important.

> Yes, and in your opinion that was a compliment.

I was looking through my notes for an idea and found "French friescream." It was either a dish, an exclamation or a Transformer. It's funny in any case.

First, have the simple decency to let the person asking the question finish without cutting them off!

So, boss, about the RJ-17 form

The Cadillac of forms!

Yeah, well, I was wondering

Why it's so awesome? Why it's everything a form should be! Long. Complex.

Filled out by people other than you.

And don't forget the tininess of the type!

Then, try to find it in your heart to acknowledge that you have, in fact, been asked a question.

What do you do with the RJ-17? You've never told me.

That's true.

If I threaten you with violence will you tell me?

Is it that important to you?

The question, no. The violence, very much yes.

A seemingly simple question can have several answers, all of them valid. Give the answer that seems most pertinent.

You fill out the RJ-17 because If you do, I'll give you your paycheck.

So you're extorting me to do it.

That's pretty pessimistic. An optimist would say I'm bribing you to do it.

Wow! Optimism isn't what it used to be.

And if you don't know the answer to the question, please feel free to say so, rather than just making something up.

Well, I send everyone's RJ-17 to corporate.

What do they do with them?

Dunno. They won't tell me.

So you're just as big a stooge as the rest of us.

Even bigger. I'm the Stooge-King. Does that make you feel better?

Yes, but like optimism, feeling better isn't what it used to be.

 The idea that your employer is either extorting you or bribing you is really depressing ... which means it's probably accurate.

Everybody wants something, and there's usually a reason we can't get it. If not, we wouldn't want it. We'd have it.

I want a Google Nexus One phone.

How much does it cost?

Five hundred dollars or so.

What does it do that your phone doesn't?

Fill me with lust.

And we men wonder why women don't respect us.

If you have internet followers, you can ask them for help, but be aware; that might cost you more than mere money.

Tell your readers. Maybe one works for Google.

That might damage my artistic integrity.

And if I drive too fast I might wreck my Ferrari.

You don't have a Ferrari.

How about this. If I make my analogy any plainer, it might insult your intelligence.

If you choose to lean on the people who follow you on the 'net, don't do it too often or for too petty a reason.

If you're gonna do this, ask for something else too. Something you've always wanted and have never been able to get.

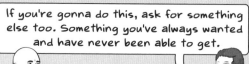

Like one of those deluxe Japanese toilet seats!

Or taste. You've clearly never had that.

If you get what you wanted, show some gratitude. Let those who helped you know that you appreciate their help.

Your idea worked!

What did you get, the phone or the toilet seat?

BOTH!

Good for you!

And I'm using them both right now!

DON'T TELL ME THAT!! I'll never feel clean again.

This seat can help with that.

GAAH!!

We live our lives surrounded by the sick and injured. Many people need medical attention without realizing it.

Before you panic, ask for details. Find out the extent of the person's problem, and how long it's been going on.

Also find out what, if anything, they've done about the problem themselves. They might have the situation in hand.

If you do advise medical attention, make it clear exactly what kind of attention, and how urgent the need is.

There are things that most people don't want to discuss at work. One example is politics, but there are many others.

I have some work for you.

I don't wanna talk about it.

You might try to have one reasonable conversation on the subject and get it over with. Good luck with that.

I find your political beliefs laughable and naive.

You don't know what my political beliefs are.

Are they different from mine?

Yes.

HA! Isn't that cute.

Or you can simply not respond. Don't take the bait. Just keep your mouth shut no matter what they say.

Wouldn't you agree that you, and all people who vote like you, are crazy?

MMMMMMMMMM!!!

Either that was a very emphatic "um-hmm," or it was a closed mouth scream.

Either one bolsters my point.

As a last resort you can try to make discussing politics with you so unpleasant that they'll avoid it at all costs.

I was saying MMMMMMM!!

It's hard to MMMMMMM!!

talk with you MMMMMMMM!!

Closed mouth screaming MMMMMMMMMMMMMMM!!

Are you trying to make me leave? UMMM-HMMMMMMMMMMMMMMM!!

 Had a coworker who constantly talked politics. I eventually wrote a disclaimer I'd read out loud if he brought it up. It shut him up. Try it!

Other people's problems have a way of becoming your problems. Specifically, because they talk about them, at you.

> My husband doesn't enjoy romantic comedies. It really bothers me.

> But he watches them with you anyway.

> You're focusing on the wrong part of the story.

> The part that makes him look good?

> YEAH!

Help them find the root of the problem. If they're going to talk about it anyway, the talking might as well be productive.

> He seems unhappy whenever we watch a romantic comedy, or go dancing, or eat at a fancy restaurant.

> So, he doesn't seem to like things he doesn't like.

> YEAH! What do I do about that?

> Buy him some acting lessons.

Try to show them the problem in a new light. You may have a new perspective that they will find helpful in some way.

> Halfway through the movie he started snoring. I sat there glaring at him as he slept for like an hour, and I thought to myself, "Is this what my future's gonna be like?"

> I'd be more concerned that that is what your present is like.

If you offer advice, make it simple, and don't be insulted when they don't listen.

> You could do things with him that he enjoys.

> But then he'll be happy, and I'll be unhappy.

> So? You're unhappy now.

> We're both unhappy now. It's balanced. That's why my marriage will last a long time.

> Or at least it'll feel like a long time.

You know you don't intend to torture your prisoner. He doesn't. The threat of torture is often as effective as the act.

Things look bad for you, Rocket Hat. But this needn't be unpleasant.

You can save yourself a great deal of pain if you'll only talk.

No deal, huh? Somehow I'm not surprised.

Describe the impending torture in minute detail. Make the anticipation of the torture worse than the torture itself.

We will use one of your Earth methods. It involves an orifice and moisture.

Yes, Earth-man, you are to be "Wet Willied!" My finger shall be moistened with my high-viscosity moon-saliva, inserted into your ear, and twisted.

I take no erotic pleasure from this act, so stop looking at me like that.

Don't be caught unprepared. Have a contingency plan in case your prisoner is unimpressed by your hollow threats.

It will be twisted in alternating directions, at varying speeds.

Your bluff's not working, Sire.

You calling it a bluff didn't help. On to "Plan B."

Let me guess, we still give him the wet willy, but using my finger.

Yes, but the saliva will still be my own.

That's most generous of you, Sire.

It's tempting to resort to violence, but in the end violence will only beget more violence, and as such, is utterly futile.

Rocket Hat fired his hat rockets at a strategic moment, resulting in a painful burn to my finger.

THE BARBARIAN!!

Could the Emperor kiss my boo-boo?

Did the burn occur before or after the ear penetration?

After, Sire.

Can't help you.

One of the few Moon-Men strips in which the Emperor does not get injured. I had to cut the line "do not underestimate the wetness of the willy."

An internet meme's an inside joke shared by everyone who's seen a video or post. As such, you'll not be the first to see it.

Tro-lo-lolo-lo

Ah, you discovered the singing Russian guy.

lolo-lo-lolo-lolololo-lo

Yeah, I'm aware of him.

lolo-lo-lolo

In fact, I'm tired of him.

Tro-lo-lolo-lo

Yup, not getting any less tired of him.

Part of the fun of a meme is getting to be the first to introduce the meme to people who haven't seen it yet.

Yi-yi-yiyi-yiyi-yi

Yiyi-yi-yiyi-yi HA-HA-HAHA!

I think he's finally cracked.

He seems happy though.

Around here, that's a sure sign that someone has cracked.

Another source of fun is discussing, mocking, or emulating the meme with others who are in on the joke.

YAAAAA-YAYA-YAAAAA

Now I'm twice as still-tired of it.

YAAAA-YAAAAA-YAYA!

Long after the meme has died you can revive it for kitsch value, or to annoy people, which is often the same thing.

One Month Later:

Haha-haha-HA haha-ha-haha-ha

Yeah, the Russian guy isn't so funny anymore.

HO-HOHO-HO!

Ah, but irritating me is. Two can play that game.

Trololololo CHOCOLATE RAIN!

If you don't know what this comic is about, google "trololo". If it had been shown on American TV when it was made, it might have ended the cold war.

Make no mistake. If you express a deeply held belief that goes against the status quo, you will suffer for it.

The angrier you are, the more easy you are to dismiss. Explain your beliefs as rationally as possible.

Don't give in. You'll face opposition, but remember, one man's "stubborn jackass" is another's "heroic civil disobedient."

Continue to point out problems and offer solutions in the face of your opponent's ridicule. In the end, reason will prevail.

I am 100% sincere about all of the opinions in this comic. Something between two of something is a sandwich. One thing on top of another thing is a pile.

In order to communicate anything important, two parties need to share mutually understood definitions.

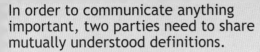

Just because something has a slice of bread under it, doesn't mean it's a sandwich.

I thought we were all done arguing about open-faced sandwiches.

Just because you stop talking and walk away doesn't mean we are done arguing.

If you identify a word in need of definition, start with a basic definition of the word on which all parties can agree.

I maintain that in order to be called a sandwich something must have a bready covering on at least two sides, and the eater must be able to easily pick it up.

Do you agree?

I don't care enough to argue.

Same thing.

Then start looking for exceptions and extreme cases that will challenge your mutual definition.

So is a hamburger a sandwich?

Obviously.

A Taco?

Yes.

A slice of pizza?

Yes, if you fold it.

Chowder in a bread bowl?

It's a soup sandwich, the world's most efficient lunch!

It's a slow process, but a necessary one. Only when both parties understand each other can there be progress.

So we agree that anyone offering an open-faced sandwich is wrong.

By your definition.

And that I have the right to feel superior to them.

Silently, yes.

What if I voice my feelings of superiority?

I'll voice my feelings of superiority.

Silently it is.

Other things I count as a sandwich. Gyros. A burrito, if it has no sauce on it, which I think is an enchilada anyway. A corndog, if you discard the stick.

Ignorance surrounds many subjects simply because discussing them makes people uncomfortable.

Young people need to learn about sexually transmitted diseases. I have an idea.

A bad idea.

I haven't even told you the idea yet.

And I wish you wouldn't. That way I can't be named as an accomplice when they arrest you.

The trick is to sneak information about an uncomfortable subject into something with which people are comfortable.

It's a game, or rather a new game board for the board game "Risk." I call it "Contamination Risk."

I take it back. You won't be arrested.

Parker Brothers will sue you back to the Stone Age long before that ever happens.

If you make the information too subtle, the information won't get across. If it's too obvious, the discomfort comes back.

The lines between the people represent possible transmission points for the viruses.

I noticed that. Some of those lines are ...

... surprising.

I'm not here to judge, just to teach.

But what are you teaching?

Your goal is to communicate information, that's all. Even if you're successful, the subject will likely remain uncomfortable.

I'm attacking from my hand to your butt.

This is a bad idea.

What, the game, or me attacking your butt with my hand?

BOTH!!

I love the games Monopoly and Risk. Nobody will play with me. I like to see these things out to the bitter end. That isn't most people's idea of fun.

Everybody has different tastes, and there are some things you just will never like.

I wrote a haiku.

I don't like poetry.

There once was a man ... from Nantucket who could not ... fit well in haikus.

Neither do you, judging by how you treat it.

But occasionally you'll find something that is a particularly well-executed example of something you do not like.

Take this job and shove it!

I'll turn off the music. I know you don't like Johnny Paycheck.

I have nothing against Johnny Paycheck. He made some bad decisions, but he had talent.

It's country western music I don't like.

That's all he sang.

Like I said, bad decisions.

People will find this confusing, but just explain that you can appreciate quality and artistry, regardless of the product.

Just because I don't like what someone's doing doesn't mean I can't tell that they're doing it well.

It's like being impressed at the amount of vomit a guy produces, or when a woman kicks you in the crotch really gracefully.

I've never had either of those experiences.

You aren't male.

Just because you don't like something doesn't mean it's bad. Recognizing this fact is a sign of maturity.

I listen to Mark Knopfler and Barenaked Ladies. They both play country-ish music sometimes.

I guess you've grown up!

And much of modern country music sounds very much like top-40 pop.

You take that back!

When writing about advanced technology or superpowers, it's easy to get bogged down in unnecessary explanations.

It is important to explain the rules and limits that govern a technology or power so it won't be seen as undefeatable.

Try to avoid detailed explanations unless there's some logical issue that is causing confusion, which you alleviate.

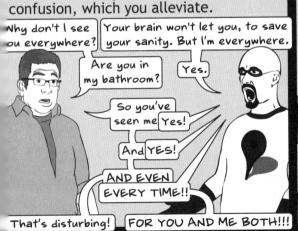

Some explanation can't be avoided, but know that this is fantasy, and too much explanation will destroy the fun.

If the last panel disturbs you, look at it this way. It's really just about me looking at my own genitalia. ... Yeah ... that didn't help, did it?

You earn your money, but that's not enough. The person who pays you needs to believe that you earn it.

How are you?

BUSY! Very busy!

You don't look busy.

You can't see it, but I'm expending a great deal of mental effort ...

suppressing ...

my urges.

Carry on.

Always walk like you're trying to get somewhere. No boss ever praised an employee for "moseying."

WOW! Better stay out of his way.

That's eight laps of the office, and I'm not too dizzy to keep going.

Your desk should be neither empty nor buried. Keep organized piles of paper on your desk and move them occasionally.

You had a stack of papers on one side of your desk yesterday, now it's on the opposite side. You know what that tells me.

What?

You're making progress! That makes me happy.

Me too.

Of course, the best way to look busy is to actually stay busy. Eventually you'll have to prove that you've done something.

What have you actually done?

My job.

And that is?

What you pay me for, and I must be doing a good job, because the alternative is for you to admit that I've fooled you.

Keep up the good work!

I intend to.

The first panel's an example of vagueness making a joke. If I told you what the urges are it'd make the joke less funny, no matter what they are.

Everybody has limits, and everybody finds them the same way. By accidentally bumping into them.

I've been watching that show Glee.

Is that the show where people just start singing for no logical reason?

They sing to express their feelings.

Like I said, no logical reason.

Once you find one of your limits, examine it. Try to find out where the actual boundary is, and why.

When they just burst into song I find it unrealistic.

Unrealistic?! Everything you watch is about robots and aliens!

But none of them sing.

What about that thing in "Return of the Jedi" with those long lip things?

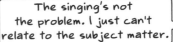

That "thing" is Sy Snootles, and she sang to please Jabba, which was a perfectly legitimate reason.

Once you've explored and defined a boundary, decide if it's rational. If it isn't, try to push through it.

Jeez, another love song.

You're just uncomfortable with your feelings.

Not true. I'm feeling scorn, with which I am perfectly comfortable.

Expanding your personal boundaries is often worthwhile, as it is one of the most fundamental forms of self-improvement.

The singing's not the problem. I just can't relate to the subject matter.

If they sang about my feelings there'd be no problem.

You want them to sing about not liking it when they sing?

Yes. I'd watch that.

Actually, so would I.

Some things are eternal. There's always a prophecy. There's always a chosen one. The chosen one's always surprised.

We believe you are the one.

The one what?

The one who is chosen by the prophecy.

Chosen for what?

Your destiny.

Well, that's vague and menacing.

Those are two of the three things that make a good prophecy.

The prophecy will include clues and signs to help the faithful find the chosen one.

Is your name a killing word?

That's stupid.

Are there midi-chlorians in your blood stream?

That's even stupider.

Do you have a lightning bolt-shaped scar?

I have a scar, but it's not where I can see it.

Let's just assume it is.

You can rebel for a time, but eventually you'll have no choice but to accept and proclaim your destiny.

I will drink the water of life, behead the Kurgan, defeat Voldemort, stop bullets with my mind, marry the girl with the jade green eyes, straighten the curves, flatten the hills, and bring balance to the force!

I am the chosen one!

And apparently, a Duke of Hazzard.

The path of the chosen one is not easy or pleasant, but you can't fight destiny.

How much cash do you have?

Why do you ask?

It is written that one shall come who will give of his wallet so that the faithful may buy liquor.

Wow. It sucks to be the chosen one.

That's the third thing that makes a good prophecy.

The works referenced in panel three: Dune, Highlander, Harry Potter, The Matrix, Big Trouble in Little China, The Dukes of Hazzard and Star Wars.

If you really don't want to discuss something, the easiest way is to simply avoid the topic.

I gotta go.

Where?

I don't wanna talk about it.

Now we must talk about it.

I see.

So, how can I actually avoid talking about things in the future?

Say that it's fascinating and start telling me. I'll either cut you off or tune you out.

Unfortunately, being vague and evasive often draws attention to the very thing you're trying to conceal.

My doctor's sending me for a test. Can we leave it at that?

Yes, but know that I'm picturing the most humiliating test possible.

And that would be?

A scrotal ultrasound.

NGAH!

I'm imagining it right now.

Please stop.

I'd like to. I really would.

If the topic comes up, lay out the facts in a frank, curt manner that says "I've given you the information, now drop it."

I'm getting my prostate checked. Happy?

Yes. I want you to be healthy.

Oh. Uh, thanks.

Does discussing it make you uncomfortable?

Well, yeah.

That makes me happy too!

You can also lie about it. Say something else happened entirely, or say that it happened to someone other than you.

You're writing a comic about Rick ...

Yes.

Getting a prostate exam ...

Yes.

Instead of doing a strip about you ...

Yes.

Getting a scrotal ultrasound.

OH YES.

All I am going to say is that somewhere there is a person who invented a conductive-gel warmer. That person should get a Nobel Prize for medicine.

A life of crime is not worth the immense downside. Planning hypothetical crimes, however, can be endlessly entertaining.

> If I were gonna steal something, it'd be that modern art sculpture that's just a urinal.

> I'd replace it with a new urinal.

> Even if I'm caught, who's gonna complain?

> Your plan is sheer elegance in its simplicity.

Crimes are interesting puzzles. You must plan what the crime is, how you'd accomplish it, and how you'd get away.

> If I were gonna commit a crime, I'd wear one of those padded suits they use to train police dogs.

> 'Cause what'll they do, sic a dog on you?

> Exactly!

> "Nice try coppers, TOO BAD I'M DOG-PROOF!"

Work through all aspects of the crime. It's great mental exercise, and the details are the fun part of the plan.

> What if they shoot you?

> That's a danger at first, but after a few seconds I'll be covered with a protective layer of police dog!

> Diabolical!

Working out an imaginary crime without the risk that comes from carrying it out is harmless fun and good for your brain.

> And my escape will be a piece of cake, 'cause nobody's gonna get in the way of a giant mass of angry dogs walking down the street.

> Especially if it's carrying a urinal.

> Exactly.

When you write about a crime, it's natural to worry some idiot might try it, but seriously, I hope someone tries this.

Men and women both feel emotions, but they process them differently. Finding a way to explain this is a challenge.
Men's emotions are like the food in a TV dinner.
A pale imitation of the real thing.
I was going to say "kept separate in little compartments," but that works too.
Describe how men experience emotions as clearly as you can. Use analogies, metaphors, or any device that may help.
We keep our emotions separate and we experience them one at a time.
So you can savor them?
No, so we can get through them as efficiently as possible and move on to something more pleasant.
Again, like a TV dinner.
List the emotions men experience regularly to give your spouse an idea of a man's emotional range.
The Salisbury steak of sadness followed by the mashed potatoes of anger followed by the apple cobbler of remorse.
Is the apple cobbler always remorse?
You've had microwave apple cobbler. What else could it be?
Helping your spouse understand your emotions will help you understand them, and show that you understand hers too.
Women's emotions are like a chicken pot pie. Everything's all mixed together, scalding hot, hidden beneath a fragile crust.
When you say things like that it makes me sooooo angry!
Would it help if I blew on you?
Absolutely not.

When faced with an angry customer, first make a sincere effort to understand their problem so you can attempt to solve it.

I'm angry.

That's understandable.

We take your money and accomplish nothing. Then when you come in to check on us, I always outsmart you and make you look foolish.

This isn't making me less angry.

That's understandable.

Next, make it clear that you are sorry. Even if you were not responsible for the problem, be sorry that it happened.

I'm sorry you came all the way down here.

Just to be disappointed?

For any reason.

Do what you can for the customer. Even if you can't fix the problem, do what you can to mitigate it as much as possible.

Would you like a Twinkie?

For what I pay your company, that'd be the most expensive Twinkie in history.

No, the Twinkie's free. You're paying us a finder's fee.

Because I found it in my desk drawer.

You might not be able to fix the problem, but you can at least make the customer feel appreciated. Try your best to do so.

I really can't apologize enough.

You haven't apologized at all!

An inadequate apology would be an insult.

No apology at all is a bigger insult.

And our customers deserve the best.

Ryan, the guy the customer's based on, is a full head taller than me. When shrunk to my size, his head looks small, which works well for the character.

104

The first thing you can do to impress people is to dress the part. Well-dressed people usually get more respect.

What are you supposed to be?

A wealthy, successful man.

You look like the Monopoly guy.

He is the most wealthy, successful man I could think of.

Oh. Then well done.

Another way to impress people is to exhibit good taste. Educate yourself about the finer things in life.

I see that like all wealthy, successful men, you're enjoying an ice-cold Big Gulp.

Don't be gauche! This, my good man, is a Super Big Gulp.

Ah yes. The Rolls Royce of "Gulps."

Quite so!

People are impressed by intelligence. Try to demonstrate reason, critical thinking, and working knowledge of fine details.

Sadly, my local 7-Eleven is unacceptable. I prefer a location that uses a reverse osmosis water filter and a higher syrup ratio.

Well, you deserve ...

What are you drinking again?

Mountain Dew, with a splash of grape Slurpee.

That. You deserve that.

Trying to be impressive isn't impressive. Your most impressive attribute is likely something that never occurred to you.

EEEEEEEEEEEEEEEEEEEEEEEEEEEEE!

What's he doing?

Shrieking. He drank his Big Gulp too fast and got brain freeze.

For a man, he's got an impressively high-pitched shriek.

THAAAAAAAAAAAAAAAAAAAAAAAANKS!

Rick is wearing a monocle under his glasses. It didn't read well on the web. It looked like he had a fancy chain attached to his glasses, which still worked.

Communication is imprecise. When people try to say something meaningful, they are often misunderstood.

A big church wedding is a lot like when they christen a ship by breaking a bottle on the prow.

What's a prow?

The front part of the ship.

Why not just say that?

I did, by using the word "prow."

Our understanding of the world is built on our experiences, and everyone's are different. Misunderstandings will result.

I get it.

It's because both ceremonies end with breaking glass.

I didn't know you're Jewish.

I'm not. I just know from experience that when your new mother-in-law threatens you with a broken whisky bottle, the wedding is over.

The best way to clear up confusion is to tell the speaker what you thought they meant and allow them to correct you.

It's because they're both empty rituals.

No.

They're both needless displays of excess.

No.

They're both primarily a photo op.

NO!

Both are a waste of good champagne.

NOT AT ALL!

Fine. Use the cheap stuff. It's your wedding.

Understanding other people is always worth the effort, as it helps us understand ourselves better as well.

I'm just saying that the marriage is brand new.

Like a newly built ship!

YES! And they're being sent off into the rest of their life together.

And like a ship, that lives will be spent performing mundane duties until they run aground or rust away to nothing.

THAT'S WHAT I'M SAYING... unfortunately.

Missy and I flew to Vegas and got married at the courthouse. There was no stress. We got fewer gifts but spent MUCH less money. I recommend it!

Life's full of people one could describe as predators. Nature has developed many ways to scare them off that we can use.

In nature, creatures that emit alarming sounds or are brightly colored are often poisonous, and should be avoided.

People don't want to tangle with me because my hair subliminally reminds them of a hooded cobra.

Or an extra from an old Burt Reynolds movie.

Eh, either way.

WANNA TALK?

No.

GOOD! I'LL TALK WHILE YOU LISTEN!

I'll be listening from several miles away.

Predators tend to avoid prey that looks obviously stricken by illness out of fear that they will be stricken as well.

Often, predators are as afraid of us as we are of them. The best way to avoid them is to make your intentions obvious.

How would you describe your ideal man?

Infection-free, for a change.

I don't want any trouble.

Good.

I just want sex. Sexy, sexy sex.

Sexy, sexy sex?

It's like sexy sex, but it's that much sexier. Interested?

Sickened. Sickly, sickly sickened.

I'd much rather be trapped with a cobra than an extra from a Burt Reynolds movie. At least the cobra's actions will be logically predictable.

We often have to explain our spouse's behavior. Sometimes your spouse's actions will defy rational explanation.

Why'd he buy a replica of the mask of Santo, "King of the Luchadores"?

I asked him that. He just said, "Es muy macho." I chose to ask no further questions.

Wise.

Other times, your spouse's actions will be rational, but still difficult to explain for social reasons.

Your wife turned down my Facebook friend request.

Why?

Is there any answer to that question that can make you a happier person?

We'll see.

Yes ... yes we will.

Of course, your spouse is an adult, and able to justify their own behavior. You can always deflect the question to them.

Why don't you ask her?

I barely know her. I've only met her, like, once.

I can see why you'd feel weird about confronting someone you barely know about their seeming unwillingness to publicly proclaim friendship for you.

Awkward, right?

The coward's way out would be to make up an explanation that will pacify the questioner and get them off your back.

She doesn't friend people she's really close with.

I see. It'd cheapen the relationship.

EXACTLY!!

When she really likes someone, she keeps it unspoken.

NEVER SPEAK OF IT!! EVEN TO HER!!

What'll she do?

SHE'LL FRIEND YOU!!

OH! I don't want that.

In any group there will be one member who lags behind the others. It is vital that this person feels included.

We are "The Legion of Super Heroes, and the Knifeketeer," a collection of the world's mightiest crime fighters. And the Knifeketeer.

I'm feeling a bit excluded.

You're included. That is what "and" means.

Make it clear that they are valued, and that their perceived inferiority is not being held against them personally.

Sorry, Knifeketeer, but to be a superhero you need a power.

I can stab.

You also need a nemesis, and all your enemies are dead.

Which proves my previous point.

Give them a chance to prove themselves. They must know that their position is not being imposed on them unfairly.

Not all of my enemies are dead. There's The Choker.

I suppose he strangles his victims.

He'd like to, but he always screws up at the last second.

It's worth the effort to be kind. One measure of a person's true worth is how they treat those less fortunate.

We shall now be known as "The Judger presents the Legion of Super Heroes: featuring Rocket Hat and special guest, Omnipresent Man.

Yeah, still feeling excluded.

I'm beginning to think your power is being unsatisfiable.

I'll admit, this entire comic exists as an excuse to get the joke in panel three out there. Nothing like a good violence pun.

Footwear takes the most punishment of any article of clothing. As such, you should give your shoes extra attention.

I stepped in some kind of poop. My socks are ruined.

Why weren't you wearing your shoes?

I was. I stepped on broken glass earlier.

It's not been a good day.

If you have a pair of quality footwear and they are damaged, consider repairing them rather than disposing of them.

I got a tube of Shoe Goo! It's like liquid shoe rubber. It sticks to your shoe and patches it.

Shame you can't put it directly on your feet.

Well I was thinking

You can't put it on your feet.

In theory I could.

Do you stay married in this theory?

If the damage is purely cosmetic, there are various products designed to repair or enhance their appearance.

The clear Shoe Goo stands out on the black shoes.

Guess you've gotta buy new shoes.

Nah, I hate shopping. I'll just cover the goo with black shoe polish.

Makes sense. Where's the shoe polish?

At the store. I should be back in a couple hours.

New shoes can be fun, but a long term relationship with a high quality pair of shoes is much more satisfying.

Behold! My shoes are now indestructible!

They look horrendous.

And they'll always look exactly this horrendous.

Brilliant! They're indestructible because they're pre-destructed.

My older brother fixed the water pump on a car by coating it with Shoe Goo. He was gonna replace it when we found a parts store, but it was working.

Nobody seeks out awkward situations, yet they seem to find us all regularly.

Have I told you about my "condition"?

No.

Well, it's AND I DON'T WANNA KNOW!

Well suffice it to say, it sucks.

I'm sure it does.

No, really, one of the symptoms is a suction in my I DON'T WANT TO KNOW!!

One common awkward situation is when the truth is obvious to everybody but the one person who really needs to know it.

This new medicine my doctor's got me on is working wonders.

Good.

It's called Placebonol. Heard of it?

Why yes, as a matter of fact I have.

Try to see the situation from every angle. More information might show you the best way to deal with the problem.

Unfortunately it's really expensive and my health plan doesn't cover it.

That's a shame ... WAIT!! YOU HAVE A HEALTH PLAN?!

You don't?

No! None of your employees do!

Oh. Well, health plans aren't so great. Mine doesn't even cover Placebonol.

Do the right thing. I can't tell you what that is, as every situation is different. You'll just have to decide what's best.

I saw a couple, and I'm pretty sure they're Smarties. It's making him look stupid, and costing him a ton of money.

But it's making him feel better.

Yes, there is that down side, but all in all, I feel it's worth it.

When I was younger, my friend's Mom had a necklace she thought was curing her arthritis. He told her about placebos. She said he was being silly.

Watching hundreds of hours of old sci-fi has taught me that eventually everyone is attacked by a fake-looking monster.

SNAKE APE!!

Oh lord.

Look at those teeth! Those arms!

Those eye holes. That zipper.

IT'S TERRIBLE!

Yes, it is.

When you are attacked by a fake-looking monster, try to defend yourself with fake-looking physical violence.

Stand back! I'm going to hit it with a two-handed over-the-head judo chop. Just like Captain Kirk.

You're gonna get the snot beat out of you.

Just like Captain Kirk.

When the fake-looking violence fails, the next move is to use pseudo-science to create a fake-looking super weapon.

I hoped I wouldn't have to use my secret weapon.

Which is clearly a hair dryer with fins glued to it.

And that's why I really hoped I wouldn't have to use it.

The last resort is to fight the fake-looking monster with another monster that's more powerful, and fake-looking.

We've been saved by Robo Snake Ape!

That's great but what if Robo Snake Ape turns on us?

We team up and perform the dreaded four-handed over-the-head judo chop.

For the last time, the Snake Ape is NOTHING like the Homestar Runner character Trogdor! Trogdor is a winged dragon with legs and one beefy muscle arm. The Snake Ape is a man in an ape suit IN A SNAKE SUIT! Why won't you listen to reason?

115

Ironically, the truly deranged seldom see a need to defend their mental state.

You okay, boss? Lately you've been acting a little paranoid.

You're working for them, aren't you?

Instead, the need to somehow prove that one is sane is most often felt by people who are mentally stable, but strange.

What the #%¢@ are you doing?

I'm drawing a Snake Ape. It has the body of a snake, and the arms and legs of an ape.

Why are you looking at me like that?

You're drawing a Snake Ape.

If someone questions your sanity, you should immediately demonstrate to them that you know reality from fantasy.

What are those black circles? Eye holes.

Why are there eye holes on its throat?

Because it's a costume. You know that Snake Apes don't really exist, right?

I knew that, and I'm relieved to hear that you know it too.

Make it clear that you are in control of your actions, and that there is a logical reason for what you are doing.

Look, I needed the dorkiest looking monster possible, and this is what I came up with.

Okay, I guess you're not crazy. Just weird.

Well I never said I wasn't weird.

That's true.

In fact, I wrote it into our vows.

Oh, I remember.

I mean, it's obvious! The Snake Ape has more arms. More hair. Trogdore has eyebrows! See any eyebrows on the Snake Ape? THEY'RE DIFFERENT!!

People talk about what they've done since they saw you. Your co-workers saw you yesterday. The topics are limited.

> Do anything interesting last night?

> I drove home. Ate. Watched TV. Went to the bathroom.

> Did you do anything I might find interesting?

> Well, in the bathroom I—

> No. The answer is no.

To enjoy the conversation you'll need a frame of reference. Find out what show they watched, and what it was about.

> It was that show where they solve mysteries.

> That's every show.

> The name of the show is an acronym.

> That doesn't narrow it down much.

> The lead guy used to make movies and there's this really hot chick who works in a lab.

> You're messing with me now, aren't you?

Listening to someone recap a show you didn't watch can be boring, but it can give you surprising insights.

> You watched a show you can't identify, where actors you can't name solved a murder that was not particularly memorable.

> That's the most pathetic thing I've ever heard.

> You listened to me talk about it for twenty minutes.

> I said it was the most pathetic thing I'd ever heard, not the most pathetic thing I'd done.

The primary reward of surviving a boring story is knowledge of how to know when you're boring others yourself.

> Then he says, "That frowny guy finds some stuff that proves that the other guy didn't do it."

> Who said this?

> The dumb guy I work with.

> They're all dumb guys at your work.

> He's the one who always wears the same clothes.

> You're just messing with me now.

> Yes. I am.

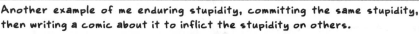

> Another example of me enduring stupidity, committing the same stupidity, then writing a comic about it to inflict the stupidity on others.

115

Occasionally we all come into contact with someone who needs some guidance.

I'm still trying to think of the best way to ask my girlfriend to marry me.

You should ask her in a way that will result in her saying yes.

What kind of advice is that?

The best kind. Inarguably true, but requiring zero thought.

Tell this person how you handled the same problem. Don't offer your solution as the best way, just as your way.

I'll never forget the day I proposed to Missy. We were standing in a jewelry store, and I said ...

"OKAY!!"

That is the least romantic thing I've ever heard.

Would it help if I mention that the Muzak was heavy on the violins?

Describe the results of your solution, so that the person you're helping can decide if it was successful or not.

So we went to Vegas and got hitched at the courthouse. Then we sent out an announcement that said in bold letters "she's not pregnant."

That's not gonna be a good story to tell your kids,

We aren't having any.

Oh. Good.

I know, right?!

Sum up your tale with any wisdom you may have gained from your experience.

The point is that you shouldn't marry her unless her idea of what's romantic is just as screwed up as yours. If it is, whatever you think will be romantic should work just fine.

That's ... good advice!

That's why my mouth is called "the wisdom hole."

Only by you.

It'll catch on, just watch.

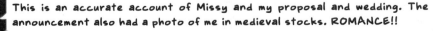

This is an accurate account of Missy and my proposal and wedding. The announcement also had a photo of me in medieval stocks. ROMANCE!!

Over time, even the most carefully managed organization will become bloated and inefficient.

Look at your organization's work flow to find parts of the team that aren't doing their job in an effective manner.

Once underperforming elements have been identified, look for ways to eliminate or replace them.

Now the hard part: have the character to make the needed changes. It will not be easy, but the benefits will be worth it.

First you must find an opportunity. Watch the world around you. Look for changes of which you can take advantage.

Once you've found a shift in society to exploit, devise a way to profit from it. The simpler your method, the better.

Don't be hasty. Examine your plan from every angle. The only insurmountable obstacle is the unforeseen obstacle.

Interestingly, opportunities (whether successfully seized or not) will spawn other opportunities ripe for seizing.

To have a worthwhile discussion with someone who has a differing viewpoint, start from a place of common ground.

Barbie's proportions are completely unrealistic.

I agree.

They've given kids unrealistic expectations.

Yup.

Everyone's been complaining about this for years. You'd think we'd have made some progress.

I guess kids aren't the only ones with unrealistic expectations.

Introduce the point you're trying to make. Try to couch it not as opposition, but as a modification of the concept.

It's not just girls. I had a Superman figure. He was muscle-bound and had perfect hair.

But it's not just Barbie's looks. It's her dream house, and her car. Her whole lifestyle's totally unrealistic.

Is Barbie bulletproof?

No.

Checkmate.

Once you've stated your point, help the other party explore your point in depth. Often they'll convince themselves.

All kids need to aim high. We don't want them to have "realistic" role models.

WHY NOT?!

Why not have kids model themselves after normal, average men and women with families and normal jobs and understandable human problems and failings?

Because you just described the Simpsons.

You win an argument not by "beating" the other party, but by coming to an improved understanding of the situation.

The problem with Barbie isn't that she's unrealistic; it's that she's silly and superficial.

They should make a new Barbie doll with depth and intelligence.

They tried. They gave her glasses and a fake book.

WOW! Shallow depth.

In fact, I think they made an episode of "the Simpsons" about it.

I considered using He-Man as an example instead of Superman. Decided against it because no boy'd call a man with a pageboy haircut a role model.

121

Well-planned parties don't just happen. Forethought has to be put into every aspect of the event, well in advance.

I need help planning a party for the staff.

What do you need me to do?

Plan the party.

Are you going to tell everyone that I planned it?

That depends. If it goes well ... no.

A party will require food. Think about how many guests you'll have and how to feed them economically.

What's it called when everyone brings food?

A potluck.

And when everyone brings their own drinks?

B.Y.O.B.

And what do you call it when that party is held in the break room?

Lunch, just like every other day.

"Party" is a verb, but not a very specific one. Have entertainment planned to give your guests something fun to do.

What about the entertainment?

They can bring games and music from home.

Are you providing anything for this stupid party?!

The planning!

I'm doing that!

And I'm providing you, ya ingrate!

But the most important item is the guest list. Planning the mix of people will help ensure that everyone has a good time.

Invite the whole staff, except you. Attending a party you planned is a conflict of interest.

Whatever.

I thought you'd be disappointed.

You would think, but knowing what this party's gonna be like, I'm betting I'll be the only one who isn't.

I've attended many an office "Drop your important work and come sing at, and give a cake to, someone who's unhappy to be aging and on a diet" party.

How to Spot the Bad Guy

Most of the fun of a good mystery is in trying to figure out "whodunnit."

> I wonder who's behind this.

> It's a mugging. I'd think a mugger's behind it.

> Gimme your wallet!

> I suspect that this goes deeper.

> Why?

> Because they don't make movies about serial muggers.

Pay close attention to anything that seems like evidence. You never know what insight will lead to the answer.

> There's your culprit!

> The wealthy old man? Why him?

> Because he's played by James Cromwell.

> That means he's the bad guy?

> Yup! He's America's favorite kindly old cold-blooded killer.

Share your theories. This gives others an opportunity to refute them, and puts your prediction on record if you're right.

> He doesn't seem like a villain.

> He never seems like a villain. That's why he makes such a great villain!

> He wasn't a villain in "Babe." He was a farmer.

> Ask the farm animals. They might have a different perspective on the meaning of the word "farmer."

Trying to guess the culprit can spoil the fun, but it makes it even more pleasant when you're surprised by the ending.

> I admit it. I'm behind it all. I knew nobody'd suspect me because I'm so old and kindly.

> I stand corrected.

> I masterminded all of the muggings. I've always loved mugging people.

> As do I.

> I see James Cromwell and I figure he's a murderer until he's proven innocent. Even in movies with no murder. I didn't trust him in Star Trek: First Contact.

121

In any situation where people are forced to deal with each other on a regular basis, someone will step out of line.

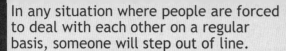

Jenkins told me I was hot. He was really creepy about it, and it made me really uncomfortable.

What did you say?

What anyone would say.

"Thanks"?

Yeah.

It's best to stay out of it, but sometimes the people involved make that difficult.

She's acting weird. Like she doesn't want to be seen talking to me.

That's how I act.

Yeah, but with her it's different. She's not joking.

I'm not joking.

HA! You kill me.

I've considered it.

It's best if you can get the offending party to tell you the story. Their version of events might prove illuminating.

I said that she's attractive.

"Attractive?"

Well, the word I used was "hot." Then I said I'd go out with her.

"Go out?"

Well, I said I'd "do" her, but going out first is just assumed! I am a gentleman.

As you clearly implied.

If you feel compelled to give advice, try to do so subtly, and use humor to cushion the blow.

There's no harm in looking.

But there is harm in looking creepy.

It's just a silly misunderstanding.

In that she's a miss, and she understood you all too well.

Nobody likes puns.

True. They're the desperate, horny men of the joke world.

Certain types of men think life is a picnic for attractive women. Ironically, they're the types who make life hell for attractive women. Just saying.

How to Help Someone See the Bright Side

If a friend of yours seems depressed, ask them why. Talking about the problem can add clarity and make them feel better.

Often people are too close to their own problems to see them clearly. An outside observer (i.e., you) can add perspective.

Find a positive aspect of your friend's predicament and re-frame the entire situation around it.

Odds are you can't change your friend's situation, but you can change how they perceive it, which can be just as good.

How to Create a Plausible Superhero Origin Story

All superhero origins are variations on a few standard stories. One of the most common is the alien who comes to Earth.

> I, the Judger, come from an alien race that sees all and judges all. I was exiled to Earth when my brethren deemed my judgments too vague, and poorly considered.

> Wow! Judged by the Judgers!

> I told them it was predictable. It did not seem to help.

Another is the hero who has no powers, but trains tirelessly to make himself something more than what he once was.

> I became the Knifeketeer by collecting a dazzling array of knives and spending many hours practicing my knifesmanship.

> But why?

> When I was a child my parents wouldn't let me have a knife. When they were slapped to death by a hemophiliac, I was powerless to save them.

When a human gains powers, it is usually through something average people don't understand well, like science or magic.

> I won my powers in a game of contract bridge.

> I didn't know you could win super powers playing bridge.

> Do you know for a fact that you can't?

> No.

> Right then!

If the means of gaining powers is easily repeatable, everyone will. That's why most superheroes get them by accident.

> And as you know, Rocket Hat gained his abilities in an accident involving model rockets, a hot glue gun and a plastic souvenir Viking hat.

> You witnessed the accident. What was it like?

> Eh, it was okay I guess. Haven't really given it much thought.

> I'm proud of the Knifeketeer's origin story. In his way, he's as hard to write for as Omnipresent Man. Turns out it's hard to make stabbing funny.

Futurists make educated guesses about the future. Getting yourself recognized as a futurist can be a challenge.

As a futurist, I feel that

Wait! Since when are you a futurist?

Since I was discovered by the foremost futurist of our generation.

You discovered yourself, didn't you?

Seeing people's potential is one of the prime talents of a good futurist.

To make predictions about the future, first look at the past. Try to find things that shape society and do not change.

Any successful new technology is driven by one or more of three human drives.

Aggression, lust, and laziness.

That's the most depressing thing I've ever heard.

But you're not denying it.

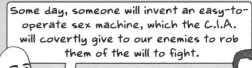

If it weren't true, it wouldn't be depressing.

Use your new insights to make sense of the modern world. Knowing where we are can tell you where we're headed.

If you could devise a service that made it safe and easy to harass your enemies or meet members of the opposite sex ...

You'd most likely violate several of Facebook's patents.

Now make solid predictions about future events and how we, as individuals and as a society, can benefit from them.

Some day, someone will invent an easy-to-operate sex machine, which the C.I.A. will covertly give to our enemies to rob them of the will to fight.

The obvious winners are the inventors, lonely enemies of the government, and the James Brown estate.

I'm gonna start opposing the government today!

There's always someone smarter than you, and many people dumber than you. They're often the ones who want to talk.

I been watching Shark Week. You been watching Shark Week?

No, I'm not really into sharks.

Neither am I.

So lemme tell you 'bout Shark Week.

You can try ignoring them. This might make them go away. More often they will try even harder to get your attention.

So the sea lion's all, "Derp derp derp."

And the shark's all, "NGAAAAAAW."

And the sea lion's all, "GUUUH!!!"

And I'm like, "Again with sharks?!" Know what I'm saying?

Yes. I'm painfully aware of what you're saying.

You could have a conversation in hopes that they'll see how silly they're being.

IT'S SHARK WEEK!! IT'S 100% SHARK!!

That's the problem. It's too sharky.

That's like saying a one pound bag of sugar is too sugary.

It is! Would you eat a pound of sugar?

SHUT UP!!

One upside of having a conversation is that occasionally you learn that they are not as stupid as they seem.

If you don't like sharks, why watch Shark Week?

Because I HATE sea lions.

Fair enough.

I swear, if someone trained a shark to build custom motorcycles, the Discovery Channel would never run anything else.

Your problems seem complicated to you. Other people's problems almost always seem much simpler.

> Cooking shows try to make gourmet food less intimidating, but it doesn't work.

> I know!

> No matter how many obscenities Gordon Ramsay screams, I don't get any less intimidated.

From your position as a disinterested observer, the solutions to other people's problems often seem obvious.

> They should do a show where they serve people steak, Jell-O and grits, and then tell them afterwards that it was filet, aspic and polenta, because really, it was.

> It'd be called "Guess What You Ate!"

> I'd never go on a show with that name, but I'd watch it every week.

Of course, if the solution really is that simple, there's a good chance someone has tried it already.

> The History Channel's so dull. They should sex it up. They could do "The History of Sex."

> That show exists.

> Then they should make it even sexier.

> "The Sexy History of Sex?"

> "Sexy Sex!" And they should work World War Two into it somehow.

Of course, unless you share your ideas with someone who can implement them, the whole exercise is pointless.

> I'll write to Food Network and suggest "Guess What You Ate." You write to History Channel with your show.

> "R. Lee Ermey's Sex Toys of the Luftwaffe." Everyone'll want to watch that!

> Heck, I can't wait to read the rejection letter!

> Then, if they got the shark to make a WWII-themed bike, and pawn it, the History Channel'd never run anything else.

When faced by an adversary, be mature about it. Make it clear that you are at odds, but avoid conflict when possible.

This is a message for the Earth man known as Rocket Hat, from me, Emperor of the Moon.

We have our disagreements, but we needn't keep fighting. I hope to settle our differences,

by destroying you in the cruelest manner imaginable.

If conflict seems unavoidable, make it clear to all that you don't seek conflict, but that you'll do what's needed to win.

There. You can't say I didn't warn you.

It would've been more sporting to warn him before capturing him.

Yes, but this was more effective, and I wasn't made Emperor because I promised sportsmanlike leadership.

If you are victorious, treat your defeated foe with respect and dignity.

Before we Moon Men dispose of our enemies we must first hold the esteem ceremony, in which we give you the respect you deserve...

...by putting on your hat, then dancing around while mocking you in a girly falsetto voice.

If you are defeated, recognize your own mistakes, and give the victor the respect and credit they have earned.

In retrospect, I should have guessed that his hat would have a self-destruct mechanism.

And it was particularly clever of him to set its trigger phrase as "Look at me, I'm Rocket Hat," spoken in a girly falsetto.

I've never liked the self-destruct mechanism as a plot device, but in this case I think it makes sense. You can't tell me you wouldn't try on the Rocket Hat.

28

Happiness is contagious. The best way to spread happiness is to act happy.

♪♪ Hmmm hmm hm hm
No tomorrow ...
hmmm hmm hm hm ♪

I didn't think it was possible to hum "Mad World" cheerfully.

Doesn't make the song any less disturbing.

No. It doesn't.

People like to feel that they are liked. When you see someone, let them know that you are happy to see them.

I'm delighted to see you.

Why?!

I just enjoy your visits.

Last time I was here you were unbelievably rude and insulting.

Yeah. That was fun.

Many situations are quite negative, but almost all situations can be explained, or "spun," in a positive manner.

We're losing clients to the competition.

Good for them! They work much harder than us, and the clients deserve better service than we give them.

You could work harder and keep our clients.

But this way I don't have to. Everybody wins.

Your emotions affect others, and their emotions affect you. The reward for spreading happiness is more happiness.

He said if we lose all our clients, he'll be fired. I told him he was being selfish.

How'd he respond to that?

Tears of joy.

He felt joy?

I did!

Tried hard to think of a song that would be both depressing and well-known. "Everybody Hurts" made me seem like a sadist, so I went with "Mad World."

131

We all have faults and flaws, but it's hard to recognize them ourselves. We need someone else to help us see them.

I think I'm just too smart for my own good.

Oh yeah! CLEARLY!

Oh, wait ... you're serious?!

I mean, uh ...

Oh yeah. Clearly.

Words are easily forgotten or ignored. To get your message across you must make them experience it in a memorable way.

This PowerPoint slide shows your intelligence as judged by me, my wife, you, society, and your ex.

Rick: The Case Against

ME   MISSY   YOU   PARENTS   EX

It looks like it's giving me the finger.

And in a sense, it is.

Be brutally honest. They need to hear the truth. Not part of the truth, or the softened version. Just the truth.

This shows all your various parts, and why women don't like them.

How many women did you ask?

Rick: The Case Against

FULL OF BAD IDEAS
STOOPED
THIN AND USELESS
SOFT & SPONGY
ATTACHED TO REST OF RICK
SUPPORTS REST OF RICK
POOR TASTE IN FOOTWEAR

One. Your ex-wife. She was quite forthcoming.

She's always happy to help anyone but me.

Helping someone doesn't guarantee they'll be grateful. They may be angry. Your reward is that they know the truth.

How would you feel if I made a PowerPoint presentation about all of your faults?

Surprised. You can't use PowerPoint.

Says who?

Ri

RESPECT FOR YOU

NUMBER OF POEMS YOU HAVE WRITTEN

Slides nineteen through twenty-three: "The big list of can'ts."

This one was a birthday gift for Ric. One of his favorite things is an early plot from Peanuts where Lucy shows Charlie Brown a slideshow of his flaws.

There comes a time in everyone's life where they face a challenge that calls for them to "bring it."

Tonight we play Monopoly. I suggest you bring it.

What, the Monopoly set?

No. I have one of those. I meant "bring it" as in "bring it on."

Oh. By it you meant "it." You should be more clear next time.

Inform your rival of the imminent delivery of the "it" you plan to bring.

Rest assured, I'll bring it. Lots of it.

"What will I do with this much of it?" you'll ask.

I'll say "Not my business. I just deliver it. If you didn't want so much of it, order less next time."

When the time is right, and the situation is most advantageous, deliver it.

Here it comes.

When?

WAIT FOR IT!!

Once you've "brought it," and they've "had it," you'll see "how they liked it."

I say "it" was victory, and I brought it to you, so technically I was telling the truth.

I suppose technically that saves your dignity.

Technically, I'm glad to hear it.

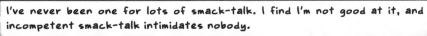

I've never been one for lots of smack-talk. I find I'm not good at it, and incompetent smack-talk intimidates nobody.

Blurting out an insult seems like a plea for attention. Casually mentioning an insult is more natural and offensive.

> Prejudice is wrong. Everyone should be treated equally.

> Agreed!

> Even people from Wisconsin.

> I withdraw my earlier statement, pending further analysis.

Clarify your opinion. Add nuance that in your mind justifies your opinion, and in others' minds will make it much worse.

> So you approve of discrimination against Wisconsinites?

> NO! Why would ANYONE EVER approve of that?!

> Exactly! There's no reason. Even if every single Wisconsinite is wrong.

> ALL OF THEM!!

Describe the situation as a clear case of right vs. wrong. Make it crystal clear to everyone which side you are on.

> They insist that their cheddar is better than Tillamook cheddar from Oregon.

> That's it? CHEESE?! That's the most trivial, ridiculous thing I've ever heard!

> I know! And yet they're just too stubborn to admit that they're wrong.

Change the subject. Smoothly shift the discussion to other issues on which most intelligent people can agree.

> And I'm not just supporting a business from the Pacific Northwest. I'm from Washington. Nothing pains me more than to say something nice about Oregon.

> Aside from cheese, Oregon's sole purpose is to filter out all but the most determined Californians.

> Well, obviously.

I got a gift basket from the Tillamook Cheese Factory after this ran. I love that place. I've taken the factory tour five times. I wish that were a joke.

A band's name is its first impression. Think long and hard about the message you want your band's name to send.

Many Years Ago:

Our band's name needs to give a sense of masculinity and power.

NARD MUSCLE!!

I hope you're making fun of me.

I wasn't, but I could start now.

RIGHT SAID FRED

Brainstorm a long list of possible names. Seek inspiration from books, movies, or anything you find meaningful.

Thieves' Forest, Miracle Max, Brute Squad.

Are all of your name ideas from "The Princess Bride?"

Yes.

Fair enough.

Princess Buttercup.

Nah, I don't like glam.

RIGHT SAID FRED

In the end, your band's name isn't nearly as important as the amount of time and effort you put into the actual music.

So, what instrument do you play?

None.

Oh. Can you sing?

Probably.

You don't care about music. You just wanna be in a band 'cause you think it'll be cool.

I'm twenty-two. That's the only reason I do anything.

RIGHT SAID FRED

Good bands are remembered for their music, regardless of their names.

And that's how Rick and I formed the world's first two-man barbershop quartet!

What did you call yourselves, "The Dateless Dans?"

"Holocaust Cloak."

Ooh! That's a cool name!

I KNOW, RIGHT?!

Dread Pirate Roberts. Gilder Frontier. Shreiking Eels. Fire Swamp. Lightning Sand. To the Pain. That movie's script is made of nothing but band names!

A team is a group of people all working together to achieve a common goal.

Our goal is to keep the client paying us while doing as little work as possible.

That's the mission statement.

Well, the rest of the staff and I have done as little work as possible. Now it's time for you to do your part.

The downside of teamwork is that often an individual will have to make some sacrifice, or "take one for the team."

Why me?

We voted.

I didn't vote.

You weren't there, but I spoke on your behalf.

What did you say?

That you wanna do it.

#@¢*%$#!

Yeah, that's representative democracy for you.

For the team to work smoothly, the sacrifices must be spread evenly so the members will perceive it as being fair.

I get all the crap jobs!

Not true! We didn't enjoy voting to hang you out to dry, and I don't like giving you the bad news.

Your sacrifice will not be forgotten.

Seriously. I'm never gonna forget this.

It can be irritating, but in the long run cooperation and teamwork are usually the best ways to achieve a difficult goal.

They haven't done anything.

Whatever. I'm just biding my time while I build a paper trail to sue your boss with.

I can help.

What've you got?

A key to the filing cabinet, and a grudge.

Welcome aboard!

Glad to be on the team.

Almost every American is sure that they know how to pronounce Oregon. A surprising number of them are wrong.

I've heard Portland or-eh-GONE is nice.

It's a great town, but you mispronounced Oregon.

No I didn't or-eh-GONE.

You're either mispronouncing Oregon, or you're butchering Maine.

In theory these sorts of problems were solved long ago, but few people really understand phonetic spelling anymore.

The accent's on the first syllable, and the o at the end is a schwa.

A schwa? What does that sound like?

"Uhhhhh."

Dude, if you don't know, just admit it.

What's more often successful is to use common words to demonstrate how a complex word should sound.

Here's how I remember. Just repeat this phrase.

I'll defend myself with a knife OR A GUN.

Ooh! That's good!

Thanks! Made it up one night at a bar in Coos Bay.

"Experts" may disagree, but ultimately the people who live there determine how a place name is pronounced.

I'd guess you'd know. You did grow up in Washington.

Eh eh eh ...

"Warshinton."

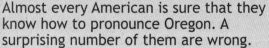

MANY Oregonians wrote me to thank me for writing this strip. NOT ONE defended Coos Bay. What's that tell you?

How to Cope with Jealousy

No matter how good you have it, someone always has it better, and that can be hard to take.

Brian May from Queen is getting his PhD in astrophysics.

It's not fair. He's great at two things. I'm barely good at one.

You're trying to figure out what I'm good at, aren't you?

Is it complaining?

Everybody is different, and it's not mentally healthy to compare ourselves to others. That said, we all do it.

He has lots of advantages I don't. Money. Fame. Free time.

Name one.

He also has obstacles you don't.

Beautiful women begging for his attention and distracting him.

Oh, that poor, poor bastard.

It's tempting to succumb to sour grapes, mocking the achievements of those who are more successful than you.

Heh, a rock star AND a scientist. Who's he think he is, Buckaroo Banzai?

Didn't you spend two years dressing like Buckaroo Banzai?

Yes, but in fairness most people thought I was dressing like Pee Wee Herman.

The only really constructive approach is to celebrate others' successes, knowing that if they can do it, so can others.

Actually, Peter Weller, the actor who played Buckaroo Banzai and RoboCop, has a master's in Renaissance art.

You're making me feel worse, not better.

Yeah, it turns out that's what I'm good at.

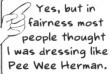

Next time someone tells you "the clothes make the man", google Buckaroo Banzai and Pee Wee Herman. The only difference is Pee Wee has a pocket square.

How to React to a Crackpot Theory

There are many crackpot theories out there. Some are old and well known, others are new and surprising.

There are still people who don't think we went to the moon.

Ridiculous!

I know, right?!

If we didn't go to the moon, how could the astronauts have had sex there?!

Simply telling someone that their beliefs are silly will not work. From their point of view, you are the one being silly.

The astronauts did not have sex on the moon.

How would you know?

Someone would've said something.

Don't be naive. What happens on the moon stays on the moon.

But they didn't send any women to the moon. Just men.

So naive.

Let the person telling you the theory explain their logic. They might surprise you by having some.

Virile young men in tight quarters. Nobody watching them. They were pioneers, and this was a chance to do something first.

You've thought a lot about this.

I'm thinking about it right now.

Please stop.

I kinda can't.

Be warned. Whether you believe it or not, often just knowing that a theory exists can forever color your perception.

We're go for manual insertion.

Time this right Jack. We only get one chance.

Can we watch something else?

I thought you liked Apollo 13.

I did.

I'm not proud of myself for making this joke. Of course, that didn't stop me.

137

If you've read either of my previous books, you know that we've reached the point where I usually include some "special features."

Usually, by "features" I mean "comics you have not seen", and by "special" I mean "already completed and easy to just slap into the book and call it a day."

Sadly, I don't happen to have any such material cluttering my desk at the moment, so what follows is all fresh material, written specifically for inclusion in this book.

Enjoy!

Fun AND LAUGHING in LAS VEGAS

A LIGHT-HEARTED JAUNT TO THE HEART OF THE AMERICAN DREAM

BANG

I found the following pages in the office printer. I believe they are part of my boss' proposed children's book treatment of Hunter S. Thompson's novel Fear and Loathing in Las Vegas.

When I asked the boss if they were his, he disavowed any knowledge of the pages, then demanded to know what I thought of them. Rather than tell you what I told him, I'm including the pages here so you can make up your own mind.

We were somewhere around Barstow on the edge of the desert when we both got the giggles.

We had Garfield books, Archie comics, rainbow wigs, noise makers Groucho glasses, Mad Libs, riddle books, a squirt flower, a joy buzzer, a whole tub of Laffy Taffy, and three books of knock-knock jokes. Not that we needed all that for the trip, but once you get locked into a serious joke-book buying binge (and you have a gift card from Half-Price Books), the tendency is to push it as far as you can.

The only thing that really worried me was the knock-knock jokes. Nothing is more helpless and depraved than a grown man telling a knock-knock joke.

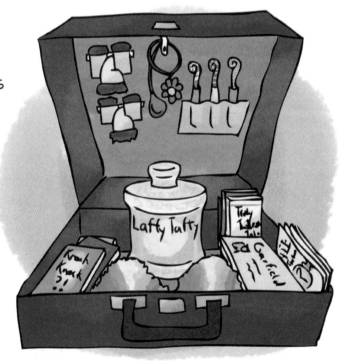

The hitchhiker's teeth were gritted.
Our vibrations were getting nasty -- but why?
Was there no communication in this car? Had we
deteriorated to the level of giddy schoolgirls?

Devil knock-knock jokes.
The only thing that's funny about them is that nobody finds them funny. So the fewer people are laughing, the funnier it becomes. The mind recoils in horror, but you're powerless to stop yourself.
It's the perfect joke for Vegas.

We had a problem in the elevator.
My attorney had made a fool of himself.

It was one of those things you heard about, but rarely saw. Book stores don't carry it anymore. The only place to get a copy is usually an older brother, or summer camp counselor.

YOU'RE NOT! *COUGH!* INDEED, ROCKET HAT DID MANY, RATHER UNPLEASANT THINGS THINGS WHILE YOU WERE ALL BICKERING. *HACK*

YOU'RE FREE TO GO.

GAH! WE MISSED IT!

I SAW THE WHOLE THING.

ME TOO, FROM MULTIPLE ANGLES.

IT WAS AWESOME!

THE END...
FOR NOW.